On The Wea

P. J. O'Rourke is the bestselling author of thirteen books, including *Eat the Rich*, *Give War a Chance*, and *The CEO of the Sofa*. He is a regular correspondent for *Atlantic* magazine.

'The great merit of O'Rourke's account is that he has absorbed both *The Wealth of Nations* and *The Theory of Moral Sentiments*, giving him a fuller and more accurate view of Smith's thinking than the stereotype.' Diane Coyle, *Independent*

'This book has plenty to recommend it. O'Rourke clearly outlines Smith's thesis, explaining the economic basis for equality, the need for clearly defined property rights and the central importance of the division of labour.' Paula Hawkins, *The Times*

'Pithy, forceful and deliberately anachronistic… A witty book.' Andrew McKie, *Daily Telegraph*

'Light but punchy, wry and impassioned, witheringly witty one moment and rambunctiously sarcastic the next… This is a judicious, finely written book.' Stuart Kelly, *Scotland on Sunday*

'O'Rourke is a reformed hippie radical who now understands the blessings of capitalism, and he offers to be our Virgil on a guided tour of what is a dense and somewhat arid book… O'Rourke has done some appreciable homework and succeeds in clarifying a couple of points that are well worth making.' Christopher Hitchens, *Sunday Times*

'With typical agility, O'Rourke shows the relevance of the 231-year-old theories via humour and popular culture… but never patronises or over-simplifies.' *Esquire*

'O'Rourke is a wonderful stylist… This book is well worth reading.' *New York Times*

Also by P. J. O'Rourke

Modern Manners
The Bachelor Home Companion
Republican Party Reptile
Holidays in Hell
Parliament of Whores
Give War a Chance
All the Trouble in the World
Age and Guile Beat Youth, Innocence, and a Bad Haircut
Eat the Rich
The CEO of the Sofa
Peace Kills

On
The Wealth of
Nations

P. J. O'ROURKE

Atlantic Books
LONDON

First published in the United States of America in 2007 by Grove/
Atlantic Inc.

First published in hardback in Great Britain in 2007 by Atlantic
Books, an imprint of Grove Atlantic Ltd.

This paperback edition published in Great Britain in 2008 by
Atlantic Books.

9 8 7 6 5 4 3 2 1

A CIP catalogue record for this book is available from the British
Library

ISBN: 978 1 84354 389 3

Designed by Richard Marston
Offset by Avon DataSet Ltd, Bidford on Avon, Warwickshire

Printed in Great Britain by CPI Bookmarque, Croydon, CR0 4TD

Atlantic Books
An imprint of Grove Atlantic Ltd
Ormond House
26–27 Boswell Street
London WC1N 3JZ

www.groveatlantic.co.uk

In hope that he will grow up in a world that enjoys the morality as well as the materiality of *The Wealth of Nations*, this book is dedicated to Edward Clifford Kelly O'Rourke.

CONTENTS

ACKNOWLEDGMENTS

It was Toby Mundy, head of Atlantic Books, London, who had the good idea for this series of commentaries. It was also Toby who had the idea (how good is not for me to judge) of asking that I write one. However the reader may feel, I am grateful for the experience. Although it did throw me into the deep end of the intellectual pool where I am not accustomed to swim.

Thanks go as well to Morgan Entrekin, chief of Grove/Atlantic worldwide, whose editorial advice ('rewrite the whole thing') was appreciated if not taken. Morgan and I have been together in that civil union known as writer/editor (and recognized by most states) since 1983. He has put every one of my books into print. Be it on his own head.

Chapter 3 of this book, on Adam Smith's *The Theory of Moral Sentiments*, previously appeared, in somewhat different form, in the *Weekly Standard*. I owe a great debt to that fine publication, which for more than a decade has let me hold forth on – anything, really, even *The Theory of Moral Sentiments*.

Another great debt (and large contribution, which is ... um, in the mail) is owed to the Cato Institute, in Washington, DC, a nonpartisan think tank promoting the individual liberty that we all love and insisting upon the individual responsibility that we don't all love quite so well. Cato is headed by President Ed Crane; its executive vice president, David Boaz, does most of the work; and I – Cato's Mencken Research Fellow – do none (being as crabby but hardly as prolific as my fellowship's namesake). Cato Senior Fellow Tom Palmer, who is a genuine Adam Smith scholar, walked me through *The Wealth of Nations*. It was Tom who pointed out that Smith, when he was using dead beavers and deer to explore the nature of value, had no idea what he was talking about. And it was Tom who noted the irony of mercantilist policy attempting to do to its own country in peacetime what it would strive to do to an enemy country in war.

Some years ago Cato offered a course of lectures, Advancing Civil Society, which are soon to be rereleased on CDs and tape cassettes. The four recordings devoted to *The Wealth of Nations* are brilliant and succinct. And listening to them is, according to an authoritative source (my wife), more pleasant than listening to me.

Julie Mariotti, with her linguistic skills and her knowledge of eighteenth-century French culture, provided me with a colloquial translation of Mme Riccoboni's letter to David Garrick. Even for someone literate in French (*je ne pas*), that missive is a nearly indecipherable jumble of obsolete grammar and long-gone slang.

James Kegley, with his knack behind the lens, provided the reader with a picture of me looking – rather inaccurately – intelligent and presentable.

I talked about my book (endlessly, I fear) to the people with whom I discuss everything that is beyond my comprehension (but rarely beyond theirs): Andy and Denise Ferguson, Nick and Mary Eberstadt, Michael Lehner, and Tina O'Rourke. The last of these, being married to the author, had to endure that talk day and night. I thank them all for their kind patience and wise ideas.

More kind patience and further wise ideas came from Ed Crane, David Boaz, Richard Starr, Philip Terzian, Richard Pipes, Charles Murray, Chris DeMuth, Toby Lester, and Cullen Murphy.

Credit must also be given to David Brooks for his reminder, in one of his excellent *New York Times* columns (they should give him the whole paper to run), that the basis of free market principles has been understood since at least the time of Albertus Magnus in the thirteenth century. And credit, too, to Robert Samuelson for his continued wonderful reporting on and analysis of economic matters. In a 2005 column in the *Washington Post,* Samuelson captured the whole of Adam Smith's argument against the know-it-alls of dirigisme and economic planning in one sentence: 'The less we understand the economy, the better it does.'

Dr William C. Freund, who was for many years the chief economist for the New York Stock Exchange, told me a joke that I have found useful to keep in mind: 'An economist is a fellow who knows 101 ways to make love and doesn't have a girl.'

I was complaining to lawyer and legal scholar Peter Huber about some of the dryness and difficulty in Adam Smith's thinking. Peter said that one may be as dull as one likes if one has something truly brilliant and original to say. This made me recall that I don't, and therefore it has behooved me to maintain a light touch with my own thinking, which I hope, but cannot promise, that I've done.

What I can promise is undying gratitude to Tina O'Rourke and Caitlin Rhodes for all the research they did and for their labors in taking what that research turned into after it had been through my mental digestive system and feeding it into the computer's maw. Thus did they keep that glowing, keyboarded troll that squats beneath the bridge of literary endeavor from devouring this Billy Goat Gruff.

I'd like to end these acknowledgments with one item for which no thanks whatsoever should be given. Cambridge University separated the study of economics from the study of moral sciences in 1903. A little soon.

He took only what his superficial mind had the power of taking, and the pith of Smith's thinking must have been left behind. To borrow even a hat to any purpose, the two heads must be something of a size.

—Adam Smith's biographer, John Rae,
on a previous author who attempted
to appropriate Smith's work

An Inquiry into *An Inquiry into the Nature and Causes of the Wealth of Nations*

The Wealth of Nations is, without doubt, a book that changed the world. But it has been taking its time. Two hundred thirty-one years after publication, Adam Smith's practical truths are only beginning to be absorbed in full. And where practical truths are most important – amid counsels of the European Union, World Trade Organization, International Monetary Fund, British Parliament, and American Congress – the lessons of Adam Smith end up as often sunk as sinking in.

Adam Smith's Simple Principles

Smith illuminated the mystery of economics in one flash: 'Consumption is the sole end and purpose of all production.'[1] There is no mystery. Smith took the *meta* out of the *physics*. Economics is our livelihood and just that.

The Wealth of Nations argues three basic principles and, by plain thinking and plentiful examples, proves them. Even intellectuals should have no trouble understanding Smith's ideas. Economic progress depends upon a trinity of individual prerogatives: pursuit of self-interest, division of labor, and freedom of trade.

There is nothing inherently wrong with the pursuit of self-interest. That was Smith's best insight. To a twenty-first-century reader this hardly sounds like news. Or, rather, it sounds like everything that's in the news. These days, altruism itself is proclaimed at the top of the altruist's lungs. Certainly it's of interest to the self to be a celebrity. Bob Geldof has found a way to remain one. But for most of history, wisdom, beliefs, and mores demanded subjugation of ego, bridling of aspiration, and sacrifice of self (and, per Abraham with Isaac, of family members, if you could catch them).

This meekness, like Adam Smith's production, had an end and purpose. Most people enjoyed no control over their material circumstances or even – if they were slaves or serfs – their material persons. In the doghouse of ancient and medieval existence, asceticism made us feel less like dogs.

But Adam Smith lived in a place and time when ordinary individuals were beginning to have some power to pursue their self-interest. In the chapter 'Of the Wages of Labour,' in book 1 of *The Wealth of Nations*, Smith remarked in a tone approaching modern irony, 'Is this improvement in the circumstances of the lower ranks of the people to be regarded as an advantage or as an inconveniency to the society?'[2]

If, in the eighteenth century, prosperity was not yet considered a self-evidently good thing for the lower ranks of people, it was because nobody had bothered to ask them. In many places nobody has bothered to ask them yet. But it is never a question of folly, sacrilege, or vulgarity to better our circumstances. The question is how to do it.

The answer is division of labor. It was an obvious answer – except to most of the scholars who had theorized about economics prior to Adam Smith. Division of labor has existed since mankind has. When the original Adam delved and his Eve span, the division of labor may be said to have been painfully obvious. Women endured the agonies of childbirth while men fiddled around in the garden.

The Adam under present consideration was not the first philosopher to notice specialization or to see that divisions are as innate as labors. But Smith was arguably the first to understand the manifold implications of the division of labor. In fact he seems to have invented the term.

The little fellow with the big ideas chips the spear points. The courageous oaf spears the mammoth. And the artistic type does a lovely cave painting of it all. One person makes a thing, and another person makes another thing, and everyone wants everything.

Hence trade. Trade may be theoretically good, or self-sufficiency may be theoretically better, but to even think about such theories is a waste of that intermittently useful specialization, thought. Trade is a fact.

Adam Smith saw that all trades, when freely conducted, are mutually beneficial by definition. A person with this got that, which he wanted more, from a person who wanted this more than that. It may have been a stupid trade. Viewing a cave painting cannot be worth three hundred pounds of mammoth ham. The mutuality may be lopsided. A starving artist gorges himself for months while a courageous oaf of a new art patron stands bemused in the Grotte de Lascaux. And what about that wily spear point chipper? He doubtless took his mammoth slice. But they didn't ask us. It's none of our business.

Why an Inquiry into Adam Smith's Simple Principles Is Not an Inquiry, First, into Adam Smith

Most things that people spend most of their time doing are none of our business. This is a very modern idea. It makes private life – into which we have no business poking our noses – more fascinating than private life was to premoderns. Adam Smith was a premodern, therefore this book is organized in an old-fashioned way. The man's ideas come first. The man comes afterward. Adam Smith helped produce a world of individuality, autonomy, and personal fulfillment, but that world did not produce him. He belonged to an older, more abstracted tradition of thought.

When a contemporary person's ideas change the world, we want to know about that person. Did Julia Child come from a background of culinary sophistication, or did her mother make those thick, gooey omelets with chunks of Velveeta cheese and Canadian bacon like my mother? I fed them to the dog. What elements of nature and nurture, of psychology and experience, developed Julia Child's thinking? But there was a time when thinking mostly developed from other thinking. The thinkers weren't thinking about themselves, and their audience wasn't thinking of the thinkers as selves, either. Everyone was lost in thought. Dugald Stewart, who in 1858 published the first biography of Adam Smith, excused its scantiness of anecdote with the comment, 'The history of a philosopher's life can contain little more than the history of his speculations.'[3]

Another reason to put the history of Adam Smith's speculations ahead of the history of Adam Smith is that Smith led the opposite of a modern life – uneventful but interesting. He was an academic but an uncontentious one. He held conventional, mildly reformist political views and would have been called a Whig if he'd bothered to be involved in partisan politics. He became a government bureaucrat. Yet the essence of his thinking – 'It's none of our business' – will eventually (I hope) upend everything that political and religious authorities have been doing for ten thousand years. In a few nations the thinking already works. There are parts of the earth where life is different than it was when the first physical brute or mystical charlatan wielded his original club or pronounced his initial mumbo jumbo and asserted his authority in the first place.

The whole business of authority is to interfere in other people's business. Princes and priests can never resist imposing restrictions on the pursuit of self-interest, division of labor, and freedom of trade. Successful pursuits mean a challenge to authority. Let people take the jobs they want and they'll seek other liberties. As for trade, nab it.

A restriction is hardly a restriction unless coercion is involved. To go back to our exemplary Cro-Magnons, a coercive trade is when I get the spear points, the mammoth meat, the cave painting, *and* the cave. What you get is killed.

Coercion destroys the mutually beneficial nature of trade, which destroys the trading, which destroys the division of labor, which destroys our self-interest. Restrain trade, however modestly, and you've made a hop and a skip toward a Maoist Great Leap Forward. Restrain either of the other economic prerogatives and the result is the same. Restrain all three and you're Mao himself.

Adam Smith's Less Simple Principles

It is clear from Adam Smith's other writings that he was a moral advocate of freedom. But the arguments for freedom in *The Wealth of Nations* are almost uncomfortably pragmatic. Smith opposed most economic constraints: tariffs, bounties, quotas, price controls, workers in league to raise wages, employers conniving to fix pay, monopolies, cartels, royal charters, guilds, apprenticeships, indentures, and of course slavery. Smith even opposed licensing doctors, believing that licenses were more likely to legitimize quacks than the marketplace was. But Smith favored many restraints on persons, lest brute force become the coin of a lawless realm.

In words more sad and honest than we're used to hearing from an economist, Smith declared, 'The peace and order of society is more important than even the relief of the miserable.'[4] Without economic freedom the number of the miserable increases, requiring further constraints to keep the peace among them, with a consequent greater loss of freedom.

Smith was also aware that economic freedom has its discontents. He was particularly worried about the results of excess in the division of labor: 'The man whose whole life is spent in performing a few simple operations ... generally becomes as stupid and ignorant as it is possible for a human creature to become.'[5] We've seen this in countless politicians as they hand-shake and rote-speak their way through campaigns. But it's worth it. Productivity of every kind can be increased by specialization. And the specialization of politics at least keeps politicians from running businesses where their stupidity and ignorance could do even greater harm to economic growth.

Adam Smith's More Complicated Principles

Smith's logical demonstration of how productivity is increased through self-interest, division of labor, and trade disproved the thesis (still dearly held by leftists and everyone's little brother) that bettering the condition of one person necessarily worsens the condition of another. Wealth is not a pizza. If I have too many slices, you don't have to eat the Domino's box.

By proving that there was no fixed amount of wealth in a nation, Smith also proved that a nation cannot be said to have a certain horde of treasure. Wealth must be measured by the volume of trades in goods and services – what goes on in the castle's kitchens and stables, not what's locked in strongboxes in the castle's tower. Smith specifies this measurement in the first sentence of his introduction to *The Wealth of Nations:* 'The annual labour of every nation is the fund which originally supplies it with all the necessaries and conveniences of life which it annually consumes.'[6] Smith thereby, in a stroke, created the concept of gross domestic product. Without GDP modern economists would be left with nothing much to say, standing around mute in ugly neckties, waiting for MSNBC to ask them to be silent on the air.

If wealth is all ebb and flow, then so is its measure, money. Money has no intrinsic value. Any baby who's eaten a nickel could tell you so. And those of us old enough to have heard about the Weimar Republic and to have lived through the Carter administration are not pained by the information. But eighteenth-century money was still mostly made of precious metals. Smith's observations on money must have been slightly disheartening to his readers, although they had the example of bling-deluged but impoverished Spain to confirm what he said. Gold is, well, worth its weight in gold, certainly, but not so certainly worth anything else. It was almost as though Smith, having proved that we can all have more money, then proved that money doesn't buy happiness. And it doesn't. It rents it.

Adam Smith's Principles: Their Principal Effect

The Wealth of Nations was published, with neat coincidence, in the very year that history's greatest capitalist nation declared its independence. And to the educated people of Great Britain the notion of the United States of America was more unreasonable, counterintuitive, and, as it were, outlandish than any of Adam Smith's ideas. *Wealth* was not light reading, even by the weightier standards of eighteenth-century readers. But it was a succès d'estime and something of an actual success. The first edition sold out in six months, shocking its publisher. Other than this, there is no evidence of Smith's work shocking his contemporaries.

For instance, Smith's suggestion of the economic primacy of self-interest didn't appall anyone. That self-interest makes the world go round has been tacitly acknowledged since the world began going round – a little secret everyone knows. And the worrisome thought that money is imaginary had been worried through by Smith's good friend David Hume a quarter of a century earlier. Indeed the fictitious quality of money had been well understood since classical times. In the two hundred years between the reigns of the emperors Nero and Gallienus, imperial fictions reduced the silver content of Roman coinage from 100 percent to none.

But, though its contents didn't make people gasp, something about *The Wealth of Nations* was grit in the gears of Enlightenment thinking. And that something is still there, grinding on our minds. I could feel it myself when the subject of self-interest came up.

Gosh, *I'm* not selfish. I think about the environment and those less fortunate than me. Especially those unfortunates who don't give a hoot about pollution, global warming, and species extinction. I think about them a lot, and I hope they lose the next election. Then maybe we can get some caring and compassionate people in public office, people who aren't selfish. If we elect an environmentalist mayor, the subdivision full of McMansions that's going to block my view of the ocean won't get built.

And let's face it, the 'lower ranks of the people' do have too much money. Look at Britney Spears. Or I'll give you a better example, the moneybags buying those châteaux-to-go on the beachfront. You with your four-barge garage and the Martha-bitchin'-Stewart-kitchen that you cook in about as often as Martha does the dishes. You may think you're not the lower ranks because you make a lot of dough, but your lifestyle is an 'inconveniency to the society' big time, as you'll find out when I key your Hummer that's taking up three parking spaces.

I know your type. All you do is work all day, eighty or a hundred hours a week, in some specialized something that nobody else understands, on Wall Street or at fancy corporate law firms or in expensive hospital operating rooms. A person has to balance job, life, and family to become a balanced ... you know, person. This is why my wife and I are planning to grow all our own food (rutabagas can be stored for a year!), use only fair-traded Internet services with open code programming, heat the house by means of clean energy renewable resources such as wind power from drafts under the door, and knit our children's clothes with organic wool from sheep raised under humane farming conditions in our yard. This will keep the kids warm and cozy, if somewhat itchy, and will build their characters because they will get teased on the street.

Okay, yes, I admit that total removal of every market restraint would be 'good for the economy'. But money isn't everything. Think of the danger and damage to society. Without government regulation the big shots who run companies like Enron, WorldCom, and Tyco could have cheated investors and embezzled millions. Without restrictions on the sale of hazardous substances young people might smoke, drink, and even use drugs. Without the licensing of medical practitioners the way would be clear for chiropractors, osteopaths, and purveyors of aromatherapy. If we didn't have labor unions, thirty thousand people would still be wage slaves at General Motors, their daily lives filled with mindless drudgery. And if there weren't various forms of retail collusion in the petroleum industry, filling stations could charge as little as they liked. I'd have to drive all over town to find the best price. That would waste gas.

Also consider the harm to the developing world. Cheap pop music MP3 downloads imported from the United States will put every nose-flute band in Peru out of business. Plus some jobs require protection, to ensure they are performed locally in their own communities. My job is to make quips, jests, and waggish comments. Somewhere in Mumbai there is a younger, funnier person who is willing to work for less. My job could be outsourced to him. But he could make any joke he wanted. Who would my wife scold? Who would my in-laws be offended by? Who would my friends shun?

This anonymous fellow, tens of thousands of miles away, might let his sense of humor run wild. He might, for example, be doing that amusing article I write about once a year concerning the trials and tribulations (and heartwarming moments) of taking the children to Manhattan at Christmastime. The kids get squashed against the glass department store windows, shoved under the tree at Rockefeller Center, and sliced to ribbons on the Central Park skating rink by hordes of Midwesterners, Europeans, and Japanese. Mumbai-Me might be tempted to slip in a bit of tasteless doggerel.

In yule New York, while suff'ring the
Ugly, rude tourist parade. A
Gift-giving thought occurred to me –
Donation to Al-Qaeda.

For the sake of accountability, sensitivity to hurtful language, and all things socially responsible, Adam Smith's flow of goods and services needs to be accompanied by at least the threat of another flow – getting a drink thrown in my face.

Then there is the matter of those goods and services – Adam Smith's gross domestic product. I am as grossly domestic as anyone. Where's the product? How come all the goods and services flow out of my income instead of into it? Of course, I understand that money isn't what's valuable. Love is what's valuable. And my bank account is full of love or something closely related to it, sex. That is, I've got fuck-all in the bank. And if money isn't worth anything, why was Alan Greenspan such a big cheese for all those years? Did he just go to his office and do Sudoku puzzles all day?

None of us, in fact, take the axioms of Adam Smith as givens – not unless what's given to us are vast profits, enormous salaries, and huge year-end bonuses resulting from unfettered markets, low labor costs, increased productivity, and current Federal Reserve policy. Like the AFL-CIO, France, and various angry and addled street protestors, we quarrel with Adam Smith. If this is to be an intelligent squabble we need to examine Smith's side of the argument in full. *The Wealth of Nations* is – as my generation used to say when my generation was relevant – relevant.

CHAPTER 2

Why Is *The Wealth of Nations* So Damn Long?

So we sit down to read, load our lap with the case-of-Scotch weight of Adam Smith's opus, and crack open *The Wealth of Nations* to page 1 of so very, very many pages. And we find ourselves in a position of intellectual embarrassment more blush-inducing than mere disagreement with Smith's logic and common sense. We face the Quantity Query. It occurs to most readers of most great works (often late at night before an exam). Even a devout biblical literalist at a conservative Baptist seminary must privately speculate upon it while wading through the *begat*s of 1 Chronicles. And I am, or on my good days I like to think I am, a devout advocate of free markets. But *The Wealth of Nations*, in my Modern Library edition, is nine hundred pages plus preface, editor's introduction, and appendix.

I've been told that one of the pleasures of middle age is getting to read the classics again, now that, almost forty years after my last college class, I've forgotten enough about them. I'm supposed to gain new, adult perspicaciousness from Plato's *Dialogues;* discover a fresh, mature appreciation of *Paradise Lost*, and experience, as a grown man, unremembered wonders in *The Wealth of Nations*. That includes wondering if I ever actually read it. I quiz myself frankly: is it the Monarch Notes that I've forgotten?

Be this as it may, another pleasure of middle age is that as the face reddens more with rum blossoms it reddens less with chagrin. I am now willing to pose the question that, as a student, I didn't have the nerve for. Imagine, in a graduate seminar on George Eliot, summoning the courage to ask, 'Why is *Middlemarch* so damn long?'

The simplest reason for Adam Smith's lack of economy with words was, aptly, economic. When *Wealth* was published it sold for one pound sixteen shillings. By Smith's own estimate the 'ordinary wages of labour'[1] at the time were ten shillings a week. Consumers, even well-off consumers of intellectual luxury goods, demand good weight. Hoist Bill Clinton's *apologia pro vita sua*, which could have been summed up in a few choice words.

The Libertarian Reader, published by the Cato Institute in 1997, did just that for Adam Smith, making his essential points in seven and a half pages of excerpts from *Wealth*. When David Boaz, executive vice president of Cato and editor of the *Reader,* was writing the introduction, he put in something to the effect that each original work from which material had been drawn could be enjoyed in its entirety. 'No, no, no, not *The Wealth of Nations*!' said Tom Palmer, senior fellow at Cato and resident expert on Adam Smith.

Smith's genius was to establish economics as a scientific discipline, distinct from the unruly jumble of the mental and material worlds that we encounter in the actual economy. But it doesn't take much of an economic encounter to bring every other scientific discipline jumbling down on our heads. Consider the psychology, sociology, political science, and mechanical engineering involved when we find that our five-year-old has left Wal-Mart with an unpaid-for My Little Pony. Adam Smith was as willing as my crying child and I are to stray from strictly economic points. Here he is, 230-odd years ahead of himself on why Angelina Jolie makes a discreditable amount of money:

> There are some very agreeable and beautiful talents of which
> the possession commands a certain sort of admiration; but of
> which the exercise for the sake of gain is considered . . . as
> a sort of public prostitution ... The exorbitant rewards of
> players, opera-singers, opera-dancers, &c are founded
> upon . . . the rarity and beauty of the talents, and the discredit
> of employing them.[2]

It is this sort of thing that makes the 892½ pages of *Wealth* that aren't included in *The Libertarian Reader* worth reading.

Or some of them. Tom Palmer isn't wrong about the slogging involved in a real perusal of *Wealth*. Not all of Smith's asides involve opera-dancers cavorting to the music of Monteverdi, presumably in scanty costumes. There is, for instance, the sixty-seven-page 'Digression concerning the Variations in the Value of Silver during the Course of the Four last Centuries'. Here yeoman service is done in the cause of quashing the idea that a certain commodity possesses a fixed value, or that we'd want it to. But to those uninterested in the historiography of currency supply, it's like reading *Modern Maturity* in Urdu.

The very largeness of his subject may have circumscribed Smith's desire to edit. And at age fifty-three, considering himself to be in poor health when *The Wealth of Nations* was published, Smith may have thought he wouldn't write another book. He didn't. Tom Palmer calls it, 'the kitchen sink effect – he had a lot to say and here was his big chance.'

The eighteenth century was a time of clarity of expression – a respite from the euphuistic blithering that went before and the romantic blather that would come after. But the Enlightenment style, though clear, was diffuse. A digression, if worthy-seeming, was not considered a distraction. It was thought of the same way twenty-first-century mothers with careers think of multitasking. And the pace of reading was more leisurely in the 1700s. There wasn't much on TV.

Edmund Burke, who could wander away from a subject with the best of them, wrote in a letter to Adam Smith, 'You are in some few Places, what Mr. Locke is in most of his writings, rather a little too diffuse. This is however a fault of the generous kind, and infinitely preferable to the dry sterile manner, which those of dull imaginations are apt to fall into.'[3]

General literacy was a relatively new thing in Smith's time, and the dry sterile manner of modern economics textbooks had yet to be dully imagined. The printed word was closer kin to the spoken word. And speaking was still a source of entertainment. Today no Michelin Green Guide would give an extra star to a restaurant that hurried its diners through a five-course meal in twenty minutes. For the same reason eighteenth-century speakers – and, by extension, writers – were not celebrated for brevity. Brevity may be the soul of wit, but *The Wealth of Nations* was no joke. Anyway, a taste for brevity is a recent fashion. Lincoln's Gettysburg Address received a tepid response at Gettysburg. And semiliterate and subliterate types still enjoy a good stem-winder on AM radio or in Hugo Chávez's Venezuela.

Smith was a practiced public speaker. He began his career, in Edinburgh, giving paid talks of the intellectually improving kind. He spent thirteen years lecturing at Glasgow University, first as professor of logic and then as professor of moral philosophy. And lecture was what he did do. Professors in the 1760s didn't just throw questions open to classroom discussion, then go around saying, 'I learn more from my students than they learn from me.' Form following function, Smith adhered to the rule of all instructional adepts: say what you will say, say what you do say, say what you did say.

According to one of Smith's pupils, John Millar, a future professor at Glasgow himself, Smith's delivery 'was plain and unaffected … As he advanced, however, his manner became warm and animated, and his expressions easy and fluent.'[4] Or, as we would put it, he talked his head off. More correctly, he could be said to have talked his head full. Smith's Glasgow lectures have survived only in reminiscences and two incomplete sets of student notes, but there is evidence he was shaping his ideas for *The Wealth of Nations* as he talked. Formal prolixity extended to his private chats. A friend of Smith's reported, 'I have often told him after half an hour's conversation, "Sir, you have said enough to make a book.'"[5] And so, at times, the book Smith made reads like an FBI wiretap transcription, except with deeper thoughts and no swear words.

'Said enough to make a book' is also a fitting comment because Smith probably dictated *The Wealth of Nations*. He claimed he found penmanship slow and difficult, and the poor script and tardy replies of his personal correspondence demonstrate it. The natural verbosity of dictation may have made *Wealth* longer, but we shouldn't complain. Most writers talk too much and often expend what brilliance they possess on their palaver instead of their writing. We have Smith's brilliance on the page, in contrast to Samuel Johnson's. We must go to that toady Boswell for Dr Johnson's lively talk, which is not so well represented in the Doctor's sometimes deadly prose and poetry.

Another reason for the expansive nature of *Wealth* was Smith's Jamesian effort to qualify his statements in order to produce the exact hue and tint of meaning he desired. Of course Smith was dealing with reality and not a male old maid's maunderings about the wispy moods of bored rich people. Plus Smith's sentences end before the cows come home. And when the end of an Adam Smith sentence has been reached, sense has been made. For example, a passage from the aforementioned digression on silver:

> Labour, it must always be remembered, and not any particular commodity or set of commodities, is the real measure of the value both of silver and of all other commodities.[6]

This can be powerfully condensed: 'Labour . . . is the real measure of . . . value.' In quoting Adam Smith, '. . .' is sometimes the most trenchant thing he said. And it may be that just such a trenchant ellipsis in *The Wealth of Nations* was what sent Karl Marx off his rocker. Notice, reading Smith's original sentence, that no grand Marxist 'value theory of labor' was created. The more so because, three hundred pages later, Smith makes the same kind of argument about food grains: 'The real value of every other commodity is finally measured and determined by . . . the average money price of corn.'[7] Smith thus maintains that work (or something akin to it, such as our daily bread) provides a sensible index for determining how much other things are worth to us. Deciding whether to mow the lawn ourselves or pay the kid next door to do it – factoring in the likelihood that he'll eat us out of house and home at snack time and run the Toro over his foot, sue us, and we'll have to get a second job to pay the legal bills – is something everybody does all the time. Marxism, as various Marxist regimes have discovered, is something nobody ever does if he can help it. (Incidentally, if the labor theory of value were true, certain children would be less worthless than they are.)

The labor that goes into a careful reading of *The Wealth of Nations* is repaid by the careful intelligence of the writing. And the reader discovers something else of value – something never hinted at by economists or scholars – Smith's sense of humor. Here is Adam Smith demolishing the notion that a nation should avoid importing goods that will be consumed and, instead, hold onto its gold and silver money, because money has enduring value:

> Nothing, therefore, it is pretended, can be more disadvantageous to any country, than the trade which consists in the exchange of such lasting for such perishable commodities. We do not, however, reckon that trade disadvantageous which consists in the exchange of the hard-ware of England for the wines of France; and yet hard-ware is a very durable commodity, and were it not for this continual exportation, might too be accumulated for ages together, to the incredible augmentation of the pots and pans of the country.[8]

Where the labor of reading *Wealth* is not always repaid is in wading through the work Smith had to do to shape his field of thought. It's particularly difficult when Smith, the lonely pioneer, is sodbusting the vast untilled prairies of econometrics. There was hardly such a thing as a reliable statistic in the eighteenth century and certainly no set of them that went back for decades. By dint of prodigious reading and protracted correspondence, Smith could find numbers to confirm his theories. But each number had to be examined for quality and weighed for usefulness in comparisons. And we have to stay there with Smith as he sorts through these apples and oranges like the world's pickiest Jewish mother at the world's worst corner grocery.

Smith then subjected numerical data to graphical analysis without the one thing you pretty much have to have to do this – graphs. The first useful graphic representations of statistics were drawn by Adam Smith's fellow Scottish economist William Playfair in 1786, in time for Smith's last revision of *Wealth*. And Smith knew Playfair, who was the young brother of a close friend. Alas, one genius didn't recognize another. Actually, two geniuses didn't. Of William Playfair's economics Jeremy Bentham said, 'Nine-tenths of it is bad writation.'[9] As a thinker, rather than a draftsman, Playfair was a tyro, but one wishes that Smith had paid attention to the callow lad anyway. Hundreds of pages of *The Wealth of Nations* that readers skim might have been condensed into several pages that readers skip entirely.

Another thing Smith didn't have, besides graphs, was jargon. Economics was too new to have developed its thieves' cant. When Adam Smith was being incomprehensible he didn't have the luxury of brief, snappy technical terms as a shorthand for incoherence. He had to go on talking through his hat until the subject was (and the reader would be) exhausted.

But the book was going to be long in any case. The Enlightenment takes its name from what, in retrospect, seems to be a cartoon moment in intellectual history. Light bulbs – except they didn't have light bulbs – appeared over the heads of people like Adam Smith. They realized that the physical world was not a divine obscurity apprehendable only by prayer and holy contemplation. In other words, they realized that not looking at things was not the best method of looking at things. If you illuminated the machinery of nature with a little observation and thought, you could see how it worked. The universe was explicable. And Enlightenment thinkers were – Prime Mover–dammit – going to explain.

Yet inexplicabilities have their comforts, and likewise, explanations have their pains. Take, as illustrations, two previously mentioned matters Adam Smith was explaining: (1) money has no objective value; and (2) money is a notation of subjective worth, because when one person exchanges something with another they both get the best side of the deal. It's not that we who are getting this explained to us are stupid. But every overcompensated modern CEO has tried the first explanation on us. And every car dealer tries the second when we offer him a trade-in.

All explanations start out brief. But pretty soon Smith gets enmeshed in clarifications, intellectually caught out, Dagwood-like, carrying his shoes up the stairs of exegesis at 3:00 a.m., expounding his head off, while that vexed and querulous spouse, the reader, stands with arms crossed and slipper tapping on the second-floor landing of comprehension.

All explanations start out brief with the exception, of course, of legal briefs. *The Wealth of Nations* is one of these as well. Adam Smith was serving a nine-hundred-page indictment of the mercantile system. Mercantilism was the dominant economic theory of his day, insofar as it can be called a theory. In fact, mercantilism was a ragbag of commercial regulations and tax and tariff policies resulting from special interest politics, influence peddling, and parliamentary logrolling all mixed together with some general misunderstandings about cash, capital flow, and government finances. Mercantilists held that the way to make a nation rich was to increase its exports and limit its imports. To give Smith's case against mercantilism in extreme concision: imports are Christmas morning; exports are January's MasterCard bill.

In *The Wealth of Nations* the accused were all the world's potentates, politicians, and wealthy merchants. But these were also the veniremen, judges, and officers of the court. Surprisingly, acquittal of the mercantilists wasn't immediate. William Pitt the Younger, prime minister during Smith's last years, accepted the evidence and instituted some reforms suggested by *Wealth*. Alexander Hamilton, architect of American protectionism, did not. More than two and a quarter centuries after *Wealth*'s publication – what with the neomercantilists running China, the opposition to globalization being voiced around the globe, and the occasional rock getting thrown through the window of a Starbucks because it doesn't foster 'sustainable development' among coffee bean growers – the jury is still out.

Meanwhile Adam Smith continues to bear witness. *The Wealth of Nations* is more than an explanation, an analysis, or an argument. It is a sermon. And a fire-and-brimstone sermon at that. Smith is famous for supposedly favoring laissez-faire (a term that appears nowhere in his writing) and for allegedly trusting the 'invisible hand' of capitalist progress. But Smith knew the hand could grasp: 'People of the same trade seldom meet together ... but the conversation ends in a conspiracy against the public.'[10]

Smith realized that a broadly prosperous consumer-oriented economy would not change human nature: 'The pride of man makes him love to domineer, and nothing mortifies him so much as to be obliged to condescend to persuade his inferiors.'[11] Truthfully, that's how we feel every time we ask to be paid for our services or goods.

Smith did believe free markets could better the world. He once said, in a paper delivered to a learned society, that progress required 'little else ... but peace, easy taxes, and a tolerable administration of justice'.[12] But those three things were then – and are now – the three hardest things in the world to find.

Smith preached against the gravitational load of power and privilege that always will, if it can, fall upon our livelihood. *The Wealth of Nations* is a sturdy bulwark of a homily on liberty and honest enterprise. It does go on and on. But sermons must last a long time for the same reason that walls must. The wall isn't trying to change the roof's mind about crushing us.

The Theory of Moral Sentiments In the Augean Stables of the Human Condition, Adam Smith Tries to Muck Out the Stalls

The unprinted subtitle of this Grove/Atlantic series on world-changing books is 'Works Which Let's Admit You'll Never Read the Whole Of'. William Kristol, editor of the *Weekly Standard* and a more erudite man than I, has a nice phrase for such tomes. He says he has 'read *in* them'. Happily, we may so do with *The Wealth of Nations*. Unhappily, there's Adam Smith's first book, which we do not read at all. And *Wealth* cannot be understood without understanding *The Theory of Moral Sentiments*, published by Smith in 1759.

Adam Smith devoted most of his career to a single philosophical project, the betterment of life. A modern reader – or a modern reader who doesn't wear Birkenstocks – is tempted to laugh. It is a hilariously big job. But many of us have undertaken hilariously big jobs such as raising children. We were lured into the enterprise by the, so to speak, pleasures of conception. New beginnings are always fun. And Smith was intellectually in bed with the virgin idea of betterment. The prospect of making wholesale improvements in ordinary life was as fascinating in the eighteenth century as the prospects of making life simpler and less stressful and of blocking e-mail spam are today.

Smith set out to discern how systems of morality, economics, and government arise and how, by comprehending the way these systems work, people could better their ethical, material, and political conditions. It was a splendid opportunity to be a blowhard. Consider a recent thinker – a Herbert Marcuse, a Newt Gingrich, an Al Franken – launching into the subject. Fortunately Adam Smith had the Enlightenment's knack for posing deep thoughts without making us cringe. His secret was to be an idealist but to not take that impertinent and annoying next step of being a visionary. Smith didn't presume to have a 'blueprint for society' and did presume that the ignorant and incompetent builders of society – he and the rest of us – couldn't follow one anyway. 'To expect, indeed,' he wrote in *Wealth*, 'that the freedom of trade should ever be entirely restored in Great Britain, is as absurd as to expect that an Oceana or Utopia should ever be established in it.'[1]

Smith chose his absurdity comparisons with an eye to the Newt Gingriches and the too visionary visions that preceded the Enlightenment. Utopia was Thomas More's sixteenth-century made-up island with people living communally and all property held in common, its name a pun on the Greek words *eutopos* and *outopos,* 'a good place' and 'no place'. Oceana was a similar locale, concocted a hundred years later by James

Harrington who mooted even more unlikely social policies such as elimination of agricultural subsidies for rich farmers and term limits. The eleventh edition of *The Encyclopaedia Britannica* calls Harrington's book, *Oceana*, 'irretrievably dull'.

The writings of Adam Smith are never irretrievably so. In book 3 of *The Wealth of Nations* there's a twenty-page passage on the Corn Laws that is a trial to read. But at the end one's fugitive attention is caught and brought back by the charm of Smith's humility in postulating an ideal. He denounced the Corn Laws, the British prohibitions on the export of grain, as the crass inequity they were (and would prove to be when they starved my family out of Rosscommon seventy years later). Then Smith *didn't* proceed with the rant that we now expect from people who feel themselves to be, a little too obviously, in the right. Instead, Smith – keeping the inevitable follies of politics in mind – came to a humble conclusion: 'We may perhaps say of [them] what was said of the laws of Solon, that, though not the best in themselves, [they are] the best which the interests, prejudices, and temper of the times would admit of.'[2]

Without this humility, reading in Adam Smith's philosophical project would be as grim as living in Kim Jong Il's philosophical project, North Korea. Smith's humble attitude extended beyond the ideal to ideas themselves, to his *amour propre*. In an early essay, 'The History of Astronomy', Smith wrote that he was 'endeavouring to represent all philosophical systems as mere inventions of the imagination, to connect together the otherwise disjointed and discordant phenomena of nature.'[3] He went on to chastise himself for agreeing too much with Sir Isaac Newton's physics, making 'use of language expressing [their] connecting principles ... as if they were the real chains which Nature makes use of to bind together her several operations.'[4] It would take, literally, an Einstein to show how right Smith was.

Adam Smith intended to publish three 'inventions of the imagination': *The Theory of Moral Sentiments, The Wealth of Nations,* and a third on jurisprudence, that is, on those most inventive and imaginary connections, law and government. The last was never finished, and just before Smith died he had his notes and drafts burned. Perhaps with reason. Many of Smith's ideas about law and government are apparent in *Moral Sentiments* and *Wealth.* The students' notes recording the lectures he gave on jurisprudence in the 1760s do not add much to the sum of Smith's thinking. Let us defer to his superior wisdom. Doing good and doing well should be enough for us. That we then should be obliged to listen to campaign speeches, make campaign contributions, and vote for fools is asking too much. As Smith himself declared in *Moral Sentiments,* 'We may often fulfil all the rules of justice by sitting still and doing nothing.'[5]

And it is from a certain kind of sitting still and doing nothing that, according to *The Theory of Moral Sentiments,* our sense of right and wrong arises. The foremost invention of our imagination is morality.

Adam Smith begins *Moral Sentiments* with the riddle upon which all our well-being depends: 'How selfish soever man may be supposed, there are evidently some principles in his nature, which interest him in the fortune of others, and render their happiness necessary to him, though he derives nothing from it.'[6] The root of these principles is, according to Smith, sympathy. We are sympathetic creatures. We possess one emotion that cannot be categorized by cynics as either greed or fear. And it isn't love. We may love without any fellow feeling, the way John Hinckley 'proved his love' for Jodie Foster.

Our sympathy makes us able, and eager, to share the feelings of people we don't love at all. We like sharing their bad feelings as well as their good ones. We enjoy, in a daytime-TV way, commiserating with the sorrows of perfect strangers. And we are so eager to have the most trivial of our own feelings shared that, Smith wrote, 'We are even put out of humour if our companion laughs louder or longer at a joke than we think it deserves.'[7]

This sympathy, Smith argued, is completely imaginative and not, like most emotions, a product of our physical senses. No matter how poignantly sympathetic the situation, we don't feel other people's pain. In a preemptive rebuttal of a future president of the United States, Smith used the example of seeing one's brother being put to the rack. (Although the brother of Roger Clinton might have chosen a more poignantly sympathetic case.) 'Our senses,' Smith declared, 'never did, and never can, carry us beyond our own person.'[8] It is our imagination that generates sympathy and gives sympathy its power.

People have the creative talent to put themselves in another person's place and to suppose what that other person is feeling.

Even very shallow and frivolous people have this creative talent. We call them actors.

But sympathy by itself – be it for humans, animals, or Clintons – can't be the basis of a moral system. Otherwise a person who watched daytime TV all day would be regarded as a saint. 'He must not be satisfied with indolent benevolence,' Smith wrote, 'nor fancy himself the friend of mankind, because in his heart he wishes well to the prosperity of the world.'[9]

Imagination, already working to show us how other people feel, has to work harder to show us whether what they feel is right or wrong. Then there's the problem of whether *we're* right or wrong. We'll always have plenty of sympathy for ourselves. 'We are not ready to suspect any person of being defective in selfishness,' Smith wrote. 'This is by no means the weak side of human nature.'[10] Morality can't be just a bunch of good feelings, or I know a pill we can swallow to be moral.

Our imaginations must undertake the additional task of creating a method to render decent judgments on our feelings and on the feelings of others and on the actions that proceed from these feelings. Adam Smith personified these conscious imaginative judgments and named our brain's moral magistrate the 'Impartial Spectator'. Perhaps this was a sly nod to the early eighteenth-century *Spectator* essays by Joseph Addison and Richard Steele in which 'Mr Spectator' made the diffident claim of taking 'no practical part in life'. That was like Oprah Winfrey saying she takes none. With the Impartial Spectator, Smith had, indeed, predicted daytime TV hosts, spreading sympathy in all directions and acting as sympathy's referees.

Of course he was technologically premature. Oprah herself would have to wait until division of labor had gone so far that we had specialists to do our imagining for us.

The Impartial Spectator produced a show for a more serious age: 'Today, utilitarian philosophers who suffer from Christian agape!' *The Theory of Moral Sentiments* is daytime TV if daytime TV were produced by PBS, featuring a host who is like Bill Moyers, except intelligent.

The host would have to be at least as intelligent as Sigmund Freud. Smith also described the operation of the superego long before Freud did, and more astutely. Smith gave it a moniker that didn't sound like a comic book hero's. And Smith connected our conscience to human attributes more noble and reasonable than what drives a miniature schnauzer to hump our leg.

We envision the Impartial Spectator as having perfect knowledge of everyone's circumstances, experience, and intentions. And since the Impartial Spectator is imaginary and has no self, it has no selfish interest in any judgment that it makes. Smith claimed that what we do, when we develop morality, is shape our natural sympathies into the thoughts and actions that we would expect from an Impartial Spectator who is sympathetic, but objective and all-knowing (and still sympathetic anyway).

'When our passive feelings are almost always so sordid and so selfish, how comes it,' Smith asks, 'that our active principles should often be so generous and so noble?'[11] The answer is 'the inhabitant of the breast ... the great judge and arbiter of our conduct'.[12] Looking at things from the Impartial Spectator's point of view instructs us in the emotional self-discipline that we need to behave even tolerably well. Consider how toddlers and drunks behave, who haven't yet received, or who have temporarily forgotten, their instructions.

Thanks to our imaginative sympathy, we are happy when other people are happy and sad when they're sad, and hope they feel the same way about us. But this emotional engagement is laborious. We have to prod our imagination to put ourselves in the place of someone who's feeling stronger sensations than we can feel – and mourn the death of a friend's ancient, stupid, leg-humping schnauzer. We have to control our own emotions when someone can't feel the sensations that we can – and laugh politely when we've taken the schnauzer's old chair and sat in the last mess it made.

According to Adam Smith, the 'wise and virtuous man' uses his imagination to create 'the idea of exact propriety and perfection'. This is 'gradually formed from his observations upon the character and conduct both of himself and of other people. It is the slow, gradual, and progressive work of the great demigod within.'[13] If, Smith wrote, the Impartial Spectator did not endeavor to teach us 'to protect the weak, to curb the violent, and to chastise the guilty',[14] then 'a man would enter an assembly of men as he enters a den of lions'.[15] Or toddlers. Or drunks. Or as he enters the set of a daytime TV show, or sits in a dead schnauzer's chair.

Adam Smith's recognition of the primary role of imagination in moral thinking reveals several things about morality. Morals are the result of effort. The proper course of moral behavior is not some piece of arcane knowledge that can be acquired by reading esoteric texts such as *Who Moved My Cheese?* Morality can't be learned by a literal reading of the Bible, for that matter. Smith pointed out that 'In the Decalogue we are commanded to honour our fathers and mothers. No mention is made of the love of our children.'[16] God didn't put it in there, because God doesn't regard us as totally unimaginative numskulls. Our sympathy for our children should go without saying. Our sympathy for our parents, on the other hand ... Did you visit Mom at Sundown Center? Or was this my week to go?

Imagining things is work. The imagination that Adam Smith describes is not the easy, whimsical one that we foist on our children, with whom we supposedly sympathize so much. There is nothing in *The Theory of Moral Sentiments* that resembles the improbably colored and far more improbably noncarnivorous tyrannosaurus on children's television. Singing along with 'Barney can be your friend, too / If you just make believe him,' leads, at best, to churnings of froth such as *Oceana*. Kim Jong Il is said to be an avid movie fan, and probably leads the imaginative fantasy life that goes with large collections of DVDs.

The imagination that Smith describes is the strenuous imagination of an Einstein or a Newton, with all the discipline that this implies. 'Self-command is not only itself a great virtue, but from it all the other virtues seem to derive their principal lustre,' Smith writes.[17] And, 'In the common degree of the moral, there is no virtue. Virtue is excellence.'[18]

This hard, creative work that imagination does links the moral sympathy central to *The Theory of Moral Sentiments* with the material cooperation central to *The Wealth of Nations*. The imagination also has to make a creative effort to divide labor and conduct trade. Sympathy and cooperation are the more-conscious and less-conscious sides of what allows civilization to exist. They are the 'principles in his nature' that man has, 'which interest him in the fortune of others'.

It applies to this man. I'm more or less conscious of when I'm being good with the family at home on the weekend, and I'm more or less unconscious at the office on Monday morning.

Smith saw the moral potential in both our interest in others and our self-interest. When we give somebody a bottle of whiskey, we know we've benefited somebody else. When the family gets to be too much for us over the weekend and we drink that bottle of whiskey ourselves, we've also benefited somebody else – the distiller, the bottler, the liquor store owner. Feeling disjointed and discordant on Monday, we don't realize this, unless we work at 'inventions of the imagination, to connect together the otherwise disjointed and discordant phenomena of nature'. The apparatus of unintended benefit was what Smith meant by the 'invisible hand', a concept he first put forth in *The Theory of Moral Sentiments*.[19]

If we don't do the difficult job that imaginative sympathy requires, we put ourselves into what Smith called 'the vilest and most abject of all states, a complete insensibility to honour and infamy, to vice and virtue'.[20] Villains are imaginative only in the public imagination. The corporate scandals of recent years may seem to be the highly inventive and original schemes of evil genius. But when the obscurities of accounting and finance are brushed aside, a prosaic hand in the till is revealed.

Policemen, prosecutors, bartenders, parents, and anyone else who has seen wrong done in large amounts can testify to Hannah Arendt's characterization of Adolf Eichmann's behavior: 'banality of evil'. Banality is the main constituent in criminal thinking – among chiselers and mopes as well as upper-echelon Nazis.

It's a mistake to read the *The Wealth of Nations* as a justification of amoral greed. *Wealth* was Adam Smith's further attempt to make life better. In *The Theory of Moral Sentiments* he wrote, 'To love our neighbor as we love ourselves is the great law of Christianity.'[21] But note the simile that Christ used and Smith cited. *The Theory of Moral Sentiments* is about the neighbor. *The Wealth of Nations* is about the other half of the equation, ourselves.

It is assumed, apparently at the highest level of divinity, that we should care about ourselves. And logically we need to. In *Moral Sentiments,* Smith insisted, paraphrasing Zeno, that each of us 'is first and principally recommended to his own care',[22] and 'endowed with the principle of self-love'.[23] A broke, naked, hungry, and self-loathing me is of no use to anyone in the neighborhood. In *Wealth,* Smith insisted that in order to take care of ourselves we must be free to do so. *The Theory of Moral Sentiments* shows us how the imagination can make us care about other people. *The Wealth of Nations* shows us how the imagination can make us dinner and a pair of pants.

Nothing but imagination could justify Genesis 1:26: 'And God said, Let us make man in our own image,' certainly not our looks. Imagination may be our only distinctively human attribute. Animals detect with their senses everything that humans do and more. Probably animals think many of the same thoughts we do, at least from nine to five. When's lunch? Animals can love. For all we know a romantic pang goes through an amoeba's heart – or whatever single cell organisms have – just before it splits. But animals, whose complete insensitivity to vice and virtue is evident when the miniature schnauzer humps your leg, cannot sympathize, let alone do so morally. Nor can animals cooperate enough to build a civilization. Unless an ant heap is your idea of the Acropolis. 'Nobody,' Adam Smith wrote in *Wealth*, 'ever saw a dog make a fair and deliberate exchange of one bone for another with another dog.'[24]

Adam Smith did not think we are innately good any more than he thought we are innately rich. But he thought we are endowed with the imaginative capacity to be both, if we're free to make the necessary efforts. *The Theory of Moral Sentiments* and *The Wealth of Nations*, read together, do provide a blueprint – though it's for the soul rather than society.

Smith never made any religious claims about his philosophical project. In a footnote to part 1 of *Moral Sentiments* he wrote, 'The present inquiry is not concerning a matter of right, if I may say so, but concerning a matter of fact.'[25] Smith meant to show, as well as his 'mere inventions of the imagination' could, only what he called 'the plan and system which Nature has sketched out'.[26] Yet the design that Adam Smith drew was for nothing less than the mechanical engineering of the Holy Ghost.

The Wealth of Nations, Book 1 How the High Price of Freedom Makes the Best Things in Life Free

Considering the immense orb of Adam Smith's thinking and his tendency to go off on tangents, *The Wealth of Nations* is surprisingly well organized. Smith divided *Wealth* into five books. He presents his economic ideas in books 1 and 2. Book 1 addresses production and distribution, and book 2 concerns capital and profit. Book 3 is an economic history of western Europe showing how various aspects of production, distribution, capital, and profit evolved and how their evolution caused a, so to speak, global warming in the climate of ordinary life. Book 4 is a refutation of economic ideas other than those of Adam Smith. It includes a particularly – too particularly – detailed attack on the mercantilists. And Book 5 is Smith's attempt to apply his ideas to solving problems of government. But since problems are the only excuse for government, solving them is out of the question. For this and other reasons, Book 5 is surprisingly disorganized.

It should be noted that Adam Smith did not create the discipline he founded. What we call economics was invented by

François Quesnay and the French physiocrats, whom Smith knew. The physiocrats, however, badly overthought the subject. Quesnay, who was Louis XV's physician, drew an elaborate Tableau Économique, a minutely labeled, densely zigzagging chart – part cat's cradle, part crossword puzzle, part backgammon board. It may have put Smith off the whole idea of graphic representation. The tableau supposedly showed how agriculture is the source of all economic progress, how trade and manufacture do no good for anyone, and how everything – from wagon wheels to Meissen chamber pots – grows, in effect, on farms. Food is the entire basis of living, therefore agriculture must be the entire basis for getting a life. So went the physiocrat reasoning, more or less.

To Quesnay and his fellow courtiers the motive for investigating economics was something between *Pour la France!* and finding a way to kill time while waiting to put leeches on royals. What Adam Smith did was give economics a reason to exist. Smith's inquiry had a sensible aim, to materially benefit mankind, himself by no means excluded.

The Wealth of Nations, Book 1

Smith called book 1, 'Of the Causes of Improvement in the productive Powers of Labour, and of the Order according to which its Produce is naturally distributed among the different Ranks of the People,' one of those people not being a modern-type book editor, who would have punched up the title.

Smith began by asking two very large questions: How is wealth produced, and how is it distributed? Over the course of the 250-some pages in book 1 the answers – 'division of labor' and 'mind your own business' – are explained. But in the meantime Smith answered two even larger questions: Why is everyone equal, and why do we have property rights?

All men are created equal. We hold this truth to be self-evident, which on the face of it is so wildly untrue. Equality is the foundation of liberal democracy, rule of law, a free society, and everything that the reader, if he or she is sane, cherishes. But are we all equal because we all showed up? It does not work that way at weddings or funerals. Are we all equal because it says so in the American Declaration of Independence, the French Declaration of the Rights of Man, and the UN Universal Declaration of Human Rights? Each of these documents contains plenty of half-truths and nontruths as well. The UN proclaims, 'Everyone has the right to rest and leisure, including reasonable limitation of working hours.' I'll have my wife inform the baby.

High-minded screeds cobbled together by unrepresentative and, in some cases, slightly deranged members of the intelligentsia are not scripture. Anyway, to see what a scripture-based polity gets for a social system we have only to look at the Taliban in Afghanistan or the Puritans in Massachusetts. Everyone has an immortal soul and every soul is of identical value to God, maybe, but that doesn't take us far as a matter of practical political philosophy. And Adam Smith was practical. His footnote to *Moral Sentiments* about how his theory was 'not concerning a matter of right ... but concerning a matter of fact' is suitable to all of his philosophy.

When Smith considered how division of labor developed, he briefly – for Smith – directed our attention to an interesting and characteristic quality of man. The most powerful creature to ever stride the earth is the most pitifully helpless. We are born incapable of caring for ourselves and remain so – to judge by today's youth – until we're forty. At the age of two when any other mammal is in its peak earning years, hunting, gathering, and procreating, the human toddler cannot find its ass with both hands, at least not well enough to use the potty. The creativity of a Daniel Defoe couldn't get Robinson Crusoe through the workweek without a supply of manufactured goods from the shipwreck's hold and the services of a cannibal executive assistant.

We must treat other people with the respect due to equals not because we are inspired by principle or filled with fraternal affection but because we're pathetic and useless.

Smith wrote that an individual 'stands at all times in need of the co-operation and assistance of great multitudes, while his whole life is scarce sufficient to gain the friendship of a few persons'.[1] This nearly left-wing statement was the prologue to Adam Smith's most quoted passage: 'It is not from the benevolence of the butcher, the brewer, or the baker, that we expect our dinner, but from their regard to their own interest.'[2] Smith wasn't urging us to selfishly pursue wealth in the free enterprise system. He was urging us to give thanks that the butcher, the brewer, and the baker do. It is our good fortune that they are endowed by their Creator with certain unalienable rights, that among these are steak, beer, and hoagie rolls.

Smith's answer to why we have property rights was equally straightforward: 'The property which every man has in his own labour, as it is the original foundation of all other property, so it is the most sacred and inviolable.'[3] Property rights are not an invention of the rich to keep poor people off their property. Property rights are the deed we have to ownership of ourselves. The property may be modest, but it is inherent. 'The patrimony of a poor man,' Smith wrote, 'lies in the strength and dexterity of his hands.'[4] From this humble grasp of hammer and, ahem, sickle, comes all free enterprise: 'and to hinder him from employing this strength and dexterity in what manner he thinks proper without injury to his neighbour, is a plain violation of this most sacred property.'[5]

Any definition of liberty that is not based on a right to property and a right to the same rights as all other people have is meaningless. What we have is ours, and nobody can push us around. This is practically all we mean when we say we are free. Other rights derive from these, when we even bother with those other rights.

Freedom of speech is wonderful, if you have anything to say. A search of the 'blogosphere' reveals that hardly anyone does. Freedom of religion is more wonderful, but you can, when you pray, 'enter into thy closet, and when thou hast shut thy door, pray to thy Father which is in secret' (Matt. 6:6). Jesus Christ himself said so. Freedom is mostly a workaday experience, taking place in the material, economic world. Before Adam Smith was even well under way with *The Wealth of Nations* he had proved that we require and deserve an equitable society where we're free from the exercise of arbitrary power and can go to the mall and swipe our Visa cards until the magnetic strips are toasted crisp, if that's what we want.

The Divisibility of Labor

However, the main purpose of Book 1 of *Wealth*, as Smith conceived it, was to show the importance of the division of labor. The purpose of division of labor, wrote Smith, is 'to make a smaller quantity of labour produce a greater quantity of work'.[6] Smith perceived that the division of labor – specialization – is the original source of economic growth.

Specialization increases economic value. As an example Smith famously used the 'trifling manufacture' of a pin. Without specialization and specialists' machinery it would take us all day to make one pin. In an early draft of *Wealth,* Smith noted that if we went so far as to dig in the iron mines, smelt our own ore, and so forth, we could 'scarce make a pin in a year'.[7] And somewhere a group of hobbyists – contactable via the Internet – is doing just that, to the irritated mystification of their wives.

The Indivisibility of Price

Smith proved his point, and should have left it at that. But here we come to an interesting difficulty in the rational consideration of economics – getting too rational with it. This is economics' original sin, a fault that has existed since economics was conceived. Any student in any Econ class knows the problem and has had to memorize various rationalizing formulae that result from – no, are – the problem.

While writing about the increase of economic value, Smith decided to delve into the concept of value itself. He tried to analyze price, and he could not. The price of something is what someone will pay for it, nothing more, nothing less, nothing else. David Hume, in a letter to Smith congratulating him on the publication of *Wealth,* praised the work but noted the error. 'If you were here at my fireside,' Hume wrote, 'I should dispute some of your principles. I cannot think ... but that price is determined altogether by the quantity and the demand.'[8] Yet, to think that went against Smith's inclination to think things through; so he thought things through anyway.

Smith decided that price had 'component parts'. He settled on three of them: labor, profits of stock (i.e., return on capital), and rent of land. Price theory is a recondite area of economics as people in the stock market, the commodities market, or the market for a house know, and as people in those Econ classrooms know to their terror. And Smith's confusions about price were even more confused than modern confusions.

When Smith was trying to put value on price and price on value he didn't have an Econ textbook to explain to him the 'law of marginal utility'. This would be postulated a century later by Carl von Menger, founder of the Austrian school of economics. Translating Econ textbook text into English, marginal utility means that we value a good only according to how much we value the specific unit of the good that we most recently consumed, not according to how much we value the good for being so good.

Smith came very close to stumbling on marginal utility when he noted that 'Nothing is more useful than water: but it will purchase scarce any thing.'[9] With an additional eight ounces of water all we get is a trip to the bathroom in the middle of the night. With an additional eight ounces of gold we get the upfront payment to lease a Lexus. Marginal utility explains why gold, vital to the life of no one except hip-hop performers and fiancés, is so high-priced.

However, the high price we pay for premium bottled water sends the law of marginal utility up the spout. That is where all price theory should go. Witness Adam Smith wrestling with his: 'If among a nation of hunters, for example, it usually costs twice the labour to kill a beaver which it does to kill a deer, one beaver should naturally exchange for or be worth two deer.'[10] Wait. Can killing a beaver, even in supposition, really be twice as hard as killing a deer? Deer can run like hell. We know where the beaver lives. It built the beaver dam. We've got the beaver's home address. Even if it does take twice as *long* to kill a beaver – wading around in the beaver pond smacking at Bucky's head with the flat side of a canoe paddle – who wants a beaver? It's not like the nation of hunters is wearing a lot of top hats. And after a long day of hunting, take your pick – a juicy tenderloin of venison or beaver soup?

There is an admitted pleasure in watching someone so much more intellectual than oneself going so intellectually wrong. Smith decided that labor was the most important component of price: 'Labour alone, therefore, never varying in its own value, is alone the ultimate and real standard.'[11] Then, within two pages, he contradicts himself: 'the real price of labour ... is very different upon different occasions.'[12] But earlier he'd written, 'The real price of everything ... is the toil and trouble of acquiring it.'[13]

Something in the fine philosophical mind of Adam Smith made him resist the mastery of the obvious. There is a statement from the thirteenth century, attributed to Albertus Magnus, that price is what 'goods are worth according to the estimate of the market at the time of sale'. But before a proposal is made to abandon the complexities of Adam Smith and go back to thinking plain old medieval common sense, it's worth considering some of the other thinking that was common in medieval times. Albertus Magnus preached the eighth Crusade, the last and most pointless. It didn't even try to go to the Holy Land. The eighth Crusade sailed, like an armed Carnival cruise, to Tunis.

Yet there was this about Adam Smith: Even when he was wrong he was smarter than other people. Perhaps he was especially smarter than those awful people who always know the 'value' of everything and are so eager to tell us its rightful price or its rightful pricelessness.

Labor is not a component of price, which doesn't have components. Things cost what they cost. But by founding the logical structure of *The Wealth of Nations* on the premise of labor – on how we divide it, on how we share its fruits, on the whole toil and trouble of our lives – Smith hit upon the material and moral necessity of our freedom.

Adam Smith, Capitalism's Scourge

Adam Smith cannot be said to have constructed the capitalist system. What he did was provide the logic of a level ground of economic rights upon which free enterprise could be built more easily. And he suggested to the builders that they use the wheelbarrow of free trade, the plumb bob of self-interest, and all the specialized tools of specialization. However, when Smith undertook to consider how free enterprise allocates what it produces – 'the Order according to which its Produce is naturally distributed' – he hit capitalism hard enough to make its boiled shirtfront roll up like a window shade.

Some acolytes of Smith might be surprised if they ever read him. He wrote that 'the oppression of the poor must establish the monopoly of the rich',[14] and that profit 'is always highest in the countries which are going fastest to ruin'.[15] About concepts such as 'full employment' Smith could make a noise like a John Kenneth Galbraith: 'If the society were annually to employ all the labour which it can annually purchase ... the produce of every succeeding year would be of vastly greater value than that of the foregoing.'[16] And Smith could follow that with a worse noise, a Thorstein

Veblen of a raspberry: 'But there is no country in which the whole annual produce is employed in maintaining the industrious. The idle every where consume a great part of it.'[17]

Adam Smith was tough on the landed gentry: 'As soon as the land of any country has all become private property, the landlords, like all other men, love to reap where they never sowed.'[18] He would have been amused to see the dukes and duchesses of England reduced to keeping circus animals and other attractions on their great estates and letting fat day-trippers waddle through their stately homes, camcording the noble ancestors on the walls.

Smith was tougher yet on the very people who, in his time, were beginning to generate the wealth of nations that he proposed to increase. Despite his friendship with merchants and manufacturers in Edinburgh and Glasgow, Smith had a cool loathing for the class:

> Masters are always and every where in a sort of tacit, but constant and uniform combination, not to raise the wages of labour.[19]

> Our merchants and master-manufacturers complain much of the bad effects of high wages in raising the price ... of their goods both at home and abroad. They say nothing concerning the bad effects of high profits. They are silent with regard to the pernicious effects of their own gains. They complain only of those of other people.[20]

The interest of the dealers ... in any particular branch of trade or manufactures, is always in some respects different from, and even opposite to, that of the public.[21]

Smith was not a fan of what would come to be called lobbying:

The proposal of any new law or regulation of commerce which comes from [merchants and manufacturers] ought always to be listened to with great precaution, and ought never to be adopted till after having been long and carefully examined ... with the most suspicious attention.[22]

The recent scandals in the US Congress concerning Jack Abramoff and his ilk would have appalled Adam Smith as much as they appall any good *Washington Post* editorial writer. But Smith, we can assume, would have had enough respect for his readers' intelligence not to feign shock.

And Smith was no enthusiast for the privatization of government functions. Concerning the East India Company and its rule of Bengal, Smith wrote, 'The government of an exclusive company of merchants is, perhaps, the worst of all governments for any country whatever.'[23]

Adam Smith, Capitalism's Champion

What made Adam Smith different from the later and more foolish critics of capitalism was that he never reasoned backward about the cause of economic disparity. 'It is not,' Smith wrote, 'because one man keeps a coach while his neighbour walks a-foot, that the one is rich and the other poor.'[24]

Smith also possessed none of the moral contempt for profit itself that would soon become the laurel wreath crowning every philosophical pretension. It crowned the pretension of Percy Bysshe Shelley, to give a comic example, and that of Pol Pot, to give a tragic one. The first insurrection in history to style itself 'communist' would occur within a few years of Smith's death. It aimed to overthrow the French Revolution's Directory, of all things. The uprising was led by François-Noel Babeuf, who took the name 'Gracchus' after Tiberius Gracchus the younger, the second-century BC radical land reformer and would-be dictator of Rome. Tiberius, predictably, was murdered by his opponents. And, predictably, so was Babeuf.

Instead of this sort of thing – sadly familiar to students of modern history – Smith wanted 'the establishment of a government which afforded to industry the only encouragement which it requires, some tolerable security that it shall enjoy the fruits of its own labour'.[25] Smith did not consider profits to be the same as 'pernicious gains'. He held that excessive profits were the result of laws that limited or guaranteed trade. A 'violent police' was the term he used for such legislative interference in free enterprise.

And even with a brutal constabulary of trade regulations, pernicious gains are to be preferred to pernicious losses. Imagine a world where we went about our daily activities deliberately intending not to profit by them – eating pebbles, wooing the furniture, getting in our car for the sole purpose of driving into a tree.

Smith saw an ordinary rate of profit not as what it ideologically is to the ideological, but as what it actually is to the profit-maker, 'his revenue, the proper fund of his subsistence'.[26] The freedoms of competition force the price the profitmaker charges for his goods to be 'the lowest at which he is likely to sell them ... *at least where there is perfect liberty'*.[27] The italics are added and the phrase cannot be underscored too heavily. Smith was fostering free enterprise, and he was also nurturing – just in time – resistance to socialism. 'Nothing can be more absurd,' he wrote, 'than to imagine that men in general should work less when they work for themselves, than when they work for other people.'[28] And when other people are 'The People' – not individuals but an abstraction – the absurdity becomes an insanity.

Adam Smith was not a modern libertarian, but he was a libertarian critic of capitalism. Problems of equality were not to be solved with more laws. In a free market, wages may be too low, but, Smith wrote, 'law can never regulate them properly, though it has often pretended to do so.'[29] Greater capitalist equality was to be achieved with greater equity capital, so that 'in consequence of the flourishing circumstances of the society, the real price of labour should rise very considerably.'[30]

Likewise the problems of free markets were not to be solved by increased regulation of those markets, but by increased freedom in them: 'To widen the market may frequently be agreeable enough to the interest of the public; but to narrow the competition must always be against it.'[31] Every law concerning commerce – even the most beneficent, such as the Pure Food and Drug Act – contains an element of narrowing the competition and should be 'examined ... with the most suspicious attention'. Congress banned cigarette advertising on radio and TV in 1970, about the same time that the entire nation got stoned on pot. Was Nixon's drug dealer behind the legislation?

Adam Smith, Capitalism's Original Money Maven

Another reason that Adam Smith defended economic freedom, and all the unpleasant questions of money that come with economic freedom, was that he understood the money. It was in book 1 of *Wealth* that Smith, with his 'Digression concerning the Variations in the Value of Silver', may be said to have deflated money, or our notion of it (or any notion that a prolonged discussion of it is interesting). Smith showed that the mercantilist attitude toward the precious metals could be summed up as: 'Premium is going for three dollars a gallon! Better fill up the car! Gas won't always be this valuable!' And Smith pointed out that questions of money aren't the questions we should be asking, because 'money is the exact measure of the real exchangeable value of all commodities ... at the same time and place only.'[32] The questions we should be asking are about how we can get to a better time and place.

The rich may be piggish, but money is not a Circe that transforms them into creatures with larger gullets than we have. 'The rich man consumes no more food than his poor neighbour,'[33] Smith wrote, referring to the reasonable prosperity of his time and place. In the unreasonable prosperity of our time and place it's the other way around. The larger the pie wagon the more likely that he or she is living below the government's officially decreed poverty level. Smith stated his meaning better in *The Theory of Moral Sentiments*, in the passage where the invisible hand was originally mentioned.* The rich, he said,

consume little more than the poor, and in spite of their natural selfishness and rapacity, … though the sole end which they propose from the labours of all the thousands whom they employ, be the gratification of their own vain and insatiable desires, they divide with the poor the produce of all their improvements. They are led by an invisible hand to make nearly the same distribution of the necessaries of life, which would have been made, had the earth been divided into equal portions among all its inhabitants.[34]

*This is not quite true. The most noted two words of Adam Smith's oeuvre were initially used in his essay, 'The History of Astronomy', probably written when Smith was in his twenties. But there he employed them in a disparaging way. Smith was noting that man has always had some understanding of physics, that 'fire burns, and water refreshes; heavy bodies descend, and lighter substances fly upwards, by the necessity of their own nature.' Smith averred that not even the ignorant ancients thought 'the invisible hand of Jupiter' was 'employed in those matters'. (EPS 49)

Smith did not intend the invisible hand to be understood as it usually is understood, as the agency by which economic liberty automatically produces economic progress. When he meant that, he said it: 'government which afforded to industry the only encouragement which it requires'. And the one other time that he used the phrase was in book 4 of *The Wealth of Nations*, in a discourse on the benefits of employing capital 'in the support of domestick industry', (W/L 456) where Smith – according to his own free trade principles – was wrong.

The economic benefits of wealth in a free market quickly overflow the humble vessel that is Paris Hilton, and they do not trickle down, they pour.

Adam Smith, Capitalism's Therapist

Smith understood the money that people have, and he understood people. Living before the social sciences had split into warring camps (or had claimed the dignity of being sciences), Smith was free to be a psychologist as well as an economist. The word *psychologist* existed in the eighteenth century, but its meaning was 'one who treats concerning the soul', or, as Smith most likely would have said, 'the imagination'. And Smith saw that the human imagination contains darker and more deeply rooted ambitions than greed for cash. In *The Theory of Moral Sentiments* he wrote:

> To those who have been accustomed to the possession, or even to the hope of public admiration, all other pleasures sicken and decay ... Place, that great object which divides the wives of aldermen, is the end of half the labours of human life; and is the cause of all the tumult and bustle, all the rapine and injustice.[35]

And of the Academy Awards and *Us Weekly*.

There is a limit to what people will do for money, but there is no limit to what people will do to go on *The Jerry Springer Show*. Money is not enough. To be called 'rich as Croesus' has never been a badge of prestige. The filthy rich king of Lydia wound up a prisoner of Persia's emperor Cyrus. It was Croesus who caused Solon to say that no man should be called happy until he is dead. Or famous.

As for death and glory, there's another ambition that leads to that, plus tumult, bustle, rapine, injustice, and *Us Weekly*. The desire for power pushes a man, Smith wrote, to 'the highest degree of arrogance ... to erect his own judgment into the supreme standard of right and wrong ... to fancy himself the only wise and worthy man in the commonwealth'.[36] Smith managed to describe not only Barbra Streisand but everyone in the world of politics.

There is no toil and trouble as bad as politics. The freedom of the market, though of uncertain fairness, is better than the shackle of government, where unfairness is perfectly certain. And there's an additional factor that makes business superior to politics. Smith saw that a free society tends to disconnect power from pelf. Referring to the Great Britain of his era, Smith wrote, 'The person who either acquires, or succeeds to a great fortune, does not necessarily acquire or succeed to any political power, either civil or military. His fortune may, perhaps, afford him the means of acquiring both, but ... does not necessarily convey to him either.'[37] And no amount of current groveling for campaign contributions makes this less true. Politics may be terribly influenced by money, but political power cannot simply be purchased in the marketplace. Ross Perot proved this, happily, as did, less happily, Steve Forbes.

Political powers are different from free market goods. This has to do with the nature of freedom, which is based on equality and self-possession. A citizen of a free country has property rights not only in 'the strength and dexterity of his hands' but in the strength and dexterity of his mind. 'And to hinder him from employing this strength and dexterity in what manner he thinks proper without injury to his neighbour, is a plain violation of ...' Voting rights in Florida in 2000, maybe? It's not that we can't be bought, it's that we own certain prerogatives that can't be sold. Our rights are, to use a term from property law that appears in the Declaration of Independence, 'unalienable'.

Another reason that political powers are different from free market goods has to do with the nature of markets. Unfettered private exchange cannot be limited – as the Chinese government thinks it can – to things. Material items are indivisible from the knowledge of how to make them and the ideas upon which that knowledge is based. All the more so, now, in an 'information age'. Free markets lead to thinking, that eternal enemy of politicians.

Book 1 of *The Wealth of Nations* is an analysis of the means by which we pursue self-interest and a critique of that pursuit. It is also a warning against pursuing what is worse. Adam Smith did not want us to be like 'the common people of England,' whom he saw as 'so jealous of their liberty, but ... never rightly understanding wherein it consists'.[38]

The Wealth of Nations, Book 2 'Of the Nature, Accumulation, and Employment of Stock' Let Adam Smith Be Your Market Guru

Investment guides and business motivational books sell in shocking numbers. The *New York Times Book Review* sends them to Coventry in the 'Advice, How-To and Miscellaneous' appendix to the best-seller list. But there in Coventry they stay, often for years on end, waxing fat and providing their authors with profits worthy of the fastest among 'countries going fastest to ruin'. These profits cause the authors of other sorts of books, such as this one, to seethe with envy and declare that the country is going to ruin indeed if investment guides and business motivational books are what sells.

The investing tips are always jejune. The motivating tomes usually are based on one more or less shrewd observation about business that is then plumped and padded, reiterated and restated until a marketable number of pages can be typeset. For instance, 'Keep in mind that your competitor is a man of layers. Don't judge him merely by surface appearances. Try to see "inside the suit," and understand both the things that make him comfortable and the things that rub him wrong.' Hence *What Color Is My Underwear?*, Cooksome Books, 230 pp., hardback, $29.95.

But here is *The Wealth of Nations* with its truly sagacious notice of every aspect of economics and its brainy commentary on all manner of financial concerns. Take an example from book 2. Hundreds of years before yuppies began installing pseudo-Palladian windows in the profusion of gables that block my view, Adam Smith warned against betting too much 'accumulation and employment of stock' on a red-hot housing market:

> A dwelling house, as such, contributes nothing to the revenue of its inhabitant ... If it is to be let to a tenant for rent, as the house itself can produce nothing, the tenant must always pay the rent out of some other revenue ... Though a house, therefore, may yield a revenue to its proprietor ... it cannot yield any to the public, nor serve in the function of a capital, and the revenue of the whole body of the people can never be in the smallest degree increased by it.[1]

What with Smith's work being in the public domain and all, there's an understandable temptation to wonder if something in the investment guide or business motivational line can't be culled from *The Wealth of Nations*. At the very least there should be material enough for one of those vade mecums for the self-admitted mental deficient, which people seem so unembarrassed to buy – *The Idiot's Guide to the Betterment of Life,* perhaps.

And it just so happens that book 2 of *Wealth* lends itself perfectly to such projects. Smith's subject is capital, where it is gotten, and how it may be employed to gain whopping returns. This is the stuff of best-sellers on a par with secret sexual techniques of the House of Windsor.

Unfortunately there's a problem. Adam Smith's advice, his how-tos, and, for that matter, his miscellanies are all addressed to the powerful figures who work as secretaries of the treasury, chancellors of the exchequer, chairmen of the Federal Reserve, and governors of the International Monetary Fund and the World Bank. This is not a mass market. On the other hand, the mighty do have sycophants, and maybe they'll all buy my book and give it to Paul Wolfowitz for Christmas.

Central Banking for Dummies

A central bank is the institution that controls the supply of a country's money. This would be a straightforward matter if it weren't for three facts: Money is imaginary. Banking doesn't involve money. And a central bank isn't a bank.

What the Heck Is *Money Anyway?*

'Money,' Smith wrote, 'is neither a material to work upon, nor a tool to work with.'[2] Money, like the Impartial Spectator, is make believe. It's a conjectural idea we have that vaguely approximates value. Using the guesswork of money lets us transfer goods and services in a way that is less cumbersome than barter and less repellent to our Impartial Spectator than theft.

Money is the offspring of division of labor and free trade. It is a contentious child. Notions of value cause arguments. This Smith pointed out in a Glasgow University lecture: 'The offering of a shilling, which to us appears to have so plain and simple a meaning, is in reality offering an argument to persuade one to do so and so as it is for his interest.'[3]

Smith wrote that 'money, by means of which the whole revenue of the society is regularly distributed among all its different members, makes itself no part of that revenue.' Being imaginary, it can't. 'The great wheel of circulation,' he continued, 'is altogether different from the goods which are circulated by means of it.'[4]

We probably shouldn't try to think too hard about the nature of money. In book 1 of *Wealth,* Smith made an opaque statement that showed the effect of such thinking: 'I am always willing to run some hazard of being tedious in order to be sure that I am perspicuous; and after taking the utmost pains that I can to be perspicuous, some obscurity may still appear to remain upon a subject in its own nature extremely abstracted.'[5]

And What Is a Bank?

A bank is an institution that doesn't deal in money. If we accept Smith's definition of value as 'toil and trouble', banks deal in toil and trouble. Banking is a clever device for storing your toil and trouble. And instead of being charged storage fees, you're compensated for engaging in excess toil and going to extra trouble.

For example say that, per book 1 of *Wealth,* you are killing a lot of deer. You're only getting one beaver for every two deer you kill but, nonetheless, you're getting more beavers than you know what to do with. Absent some system of banking, you have to pile the beavers under your bed where they're of no use to anyone. And they stink. Banking allows you to rent the beavers to me with 'some tolerable security' of receiving the agreed upon beaver lease revenue and getting your beavers back when I'm finished with my high-profit, beaver-intensive business deal. Money doesn't come into it except insofar as the transaction is more convenient and pleasant if it's conducted in money instead of used beavers.

'It is not by augmenting the capital of the country,' Smith declared, 'but by rendering a greater part of that capital active and productive ... that the most judicious operations of banking can increase the industry of the country.'[6] What the judicious operations of banking *can't* do is increase the *industriousness* of the country – for instance by lending money to any fool, such as me, who comes along with a lunatic idea for alternative energy technology based on methane production from rotting beavers. Political advocates of 'economic stimulus' often claim that banks ought to do this. And bankers often claim that they've done it. But they shouldn't, and they can't.

There was a banking crisis in Scotland in 1772. Only three of Edinburgh's thirty private banks survived. Every time and place has its equivalent to dot.com-boom, Silicon Valley start-ups. Adam Smith described the attitude of investors in 1999 as well as in 1772: 'The banks, they seem to have thought, were in honour bound to supply ... them with all the capital which they wanted to trade with.'[7]

So What Are Banks Really Good For?

They're good for make-believe. Banks are as imaginary as the dollars they lend. Their pillared porticos, their impressive vaults, and their handy time and temperature signs, are just symbols. The symbols represent something else we've made up called 'contract'.

It's fortunate that Adam Smith was free to be a psychologist as well as an economist. Any examination of economics quickly turns into a session on the couch, with dreams to analyze, narcissisms to probe, and family conflicts to be resolved. Money is the child of division of labor and freedom of trade, an active little bastard conceived while we were enjoying some subconscious cooperation. The wedding of property rights to equality before the law also produces an offspring, more widely recognized as legitimate than money, known as valid and binding contract. Bad banking is a bad marriage where contract is being spoiled by the selfishness of private property and the failure of equal rights to assert herself. 'When the law,' wrote Smith, 'does not enforce the performance of contracts, it puts all borrowers nearly upon the same footing with bankrupts or people of doubtful credit.'[8] Counseling should be sought. Otherwise poor little contract may start associating with the wrong element, get corrupted by money, and grow up with low self-esteem and self-destructive tendencies. This is what happened to America's Social Security trust fund.

So We Need to, Like, Regulate Banks

Freedom cannot exist without limitation. Adam Smith was not a man to flinch at this conundrum. In his consideration of banking Smith stated his most fundamental free market principle: 'If any branch of trade, or any division of labour, be advantageous to the public, the freer and more general the competition, it will always be the more so.'[9] However, in his consideration of banking, Smith also stated his most fundamental caveat to that principle: 'But those exertions of the natural liberty of a few individuals, which might endanger the security of the whole society, are, and ought to be, restrained by the laws of all governments.'[10]

So much is sensible, although you'd never know it to hear the senseless arguments between lawmakers who believe one of these ideas and lawmakers who believe the other. Unlike most politicians Smith was usually able to make his way past the sirens of authoritarianism and the sirens of license without having a head full of wax or needing to be tied to the mast. Smith had a clearer idea of the purpose of law than legislators do. He didn't see writing laws as a contest or a compromise between battling interest groups. He saw writing laws as a way of furthering 'that natural liberty which it is the proper business of law, not to infringe, but to support'.[11]

Sometimes we get that kind of law. And when we do, a lot of bankers go to jail.

What Is a 'Central' Bank?

You can't get a debit card that draws on the Federal Reserve Bank, nice as that would be, and never mind that the Bush administration apparently can. A central bank is not really a bank at all but a government agency. Smith called it 'a great engine of state'.[12] It regulates the amount of money in circulation by, basically, regulating real banks. A nation's currency supply is supposed to be matched to that nation's supply of economic value. If a nation has less circulating money than it has labor and goods, you get a credit collapse and a Great Depression. If a nation has more money than it has labor and goods, you get the 1970s. Which is worse depends upon whether you are more annoyed by double knit, disco, and Henry Kissinger or by claptrap about the Greatest Generation, enormous Medicare expenditures, and your parents.

The purpose of central banking is to prevent the return of disco and to get your parents to shut up. The technical mechanisms by which a central bank does that are beyond the scope of this book, not to mention the understanding of this writer. You actually are a dummy if you think you're going to plumb the mysteries of central banking here. The importance of what Adam Smith wrote about central banks was that Smith, as usual, understood the practical principles behind the mystery. He realized that money was not a government asset, but a government liability. He called it 'that great but expensive instrument

of commerce'.[13] And noted that 'the stock of money which circulates in any country must require a certain expence, first to
collect it, and afterwards to support it.'[14]

The Adam Smith Plan for Increased Wealth (of Nations):
How Central Banks Can Use Paper Money to Make
the Great Instrument of Commerce Work Cheap

The 'certain expence' of having a handy medium of exchange
made Smith an early advocate of paper money. Not only are
precious metals costly to mine, transport, and mint; precious
metals also have a real – not just a monetary – value in manufacturing and industry.

Smith went almost literary on the subject. He wrote that 'gold
and silver money' could be 'compared to a highway, which,
while it circulates and carries to market all the grass and corn of
the country, produces itself not a single pile of either'.[15] Paper
money would, 'by providing, if I may be allowed so violent
a metaphor, a sort of waggon-way through the air, enable the
country to convert, as it were, a great part of its highways into
good pastures and cornfields'.[16] (Although now that we really
do have a 'waggon-way through the air', not many of our in-
terstates have been turned into pastures and cornfields.)

Money is information. In his advocacy of paper money Smith
was foreseeing the virtual aspect of the modern economy and all
the efficiency that comes from it. Why buy a pricey slab of granite
and have information chiseled into it by skilled workmen when
information can be encoded almost effortlessly in the ether?

Smith was aware of the danger in what he called 'the

Dædalian wings of paper money'.[17] He was an honest and sane early advocate of paper money, which was not usual. Many eighteenth-century paper money promoters favored paper not because they thought it made money more efficient but because they thought it made money free. The most famous of these was a fellow Scot, John Law. Law proposed a national bank of Scotland which, as Smith put it, 'he seems to have imagined might issue paper to the amount of the whole value of all the lands in the country'.[18] The Scottish parliament demurred. Law went to Paris and in 1717 concocted the Mississippi Scheme along the same lines. Smith gave a detailed account of Law's operations in a Glasgow University lecture. 'The greatest part of the people,' he said, 'had their whole fortunes in notes and were reduced to a state of beggary.'[19] And in *Wealth of Nations,* Smith declared that 'the paper currencies of North America' were 'a scheme of fraudulent debtors to cheat their creditors'.[20]

Many paper currencies issued by many central banks are no better nowadays. Would you like your change in Argentinian pesos? All modern money is paper money but with nothing ensuring its relative value except the promises of a government or, in the case of the euro, the even more nebulous promises of a bunch of governments. We have our paper, or 'fiat', money because it's easier for our governments to print more of it in the name of 'greater monetary policy flexibility'. The quality of money, like the quality of the human body after the age of eighteen, is not often improved by increases in quantity. Smith wrote that 'paper money does not *necessarily* increase the quantity of the whole currency.'[21] Italics added, alas. In February 2006, Zimbabwe's reserve bank introduced a new fifty-thousand-dollar bank note, and it was not worth enough to buy a beer.

Smith proposed various intelligent limitations on central banking's paper currencies. None of them are of interest to us today because fiat money was beyond even Adam Smith's powers of conception. He thought that money would always be on a gold standard or a silver standard or a standard of some kind. (When, as mentioned before, Smith wrote about the price of food grains determining 'the real value of all other commodities',[22] he was in effect suggesting a 'market basket' of consumer goods as a currency standard.)

The worth of fiat money is linked to political whims far less substantive than John Law's 'value of all the lands in the country'. Modern governments have taken the Mississippi Scheme and made it work. Except, of course, when it doesn't.

So There Are Limitations to What Private Banks and Central Banks Can Do to Improve the Economy, but Can't Institutions Like the World Bank Provide the Economic Stimulus We Need to Eliminate Poverty and Aid Developing Nations?

No. Smith put this forcefully in book 4 of *Wealth:* 'I have never known much good done by those who affected to trade for the public good.'[23] The explanation for that grouchy outburst is in book 2 where Smith described the Ayr Bank, the collapse of which led to the 1772 Edinburgh banking crisis. 'It was the avowed principle of this bank to advance ... capital which was to be employed in those improvements of which the returns are the most slow and distant.'[24] This being what the World Bank tries to do. 'The operations of this bank,' Smith continued, 'seem to have produced effects quite opposite to those which were intended.'[25] That being how things turn out for the World Bank. Smith wrote that the wonderfully named Ayr Bank 'no doubt, gave some temporary relief ... But it thereby only enabled [its borrowers] to get so much deeper into debt, so that when ruin came, it fell so much the heavier.'[26] And there was no Bono in those days to put everything right.

Owing money to beneficent organizations is not beneficial. It's better to owe money to your scowling uncle or the skin-flint down the street. Borrowers are debtors, after all. 'The sober and frugal debtors of private persons,' Smith observed, 'would be more likely to employ the money borrowed in sober undertakings ... which, though they might have less of the grand and the marvellous, would have more of the solid and the profitable.'[27] This maxim applies to everything from programs of foreign aid in the developing world to local city council debates. One new hot dog vendor is better for a town than any number of municipally financed sports sta-diums. Smith declared that if the Ayr Bank had succeeded it still would have been a failure, that 'this operation, therefore, without increasing in the smallest degree the capital of the country, would only have transferred a great part of it from prudent and profitable, to imprudent and unprofitable undertakings.'[28]

A recurring lesson in *The Wealth of Nations* is that we shouldn't get greedy. And no people are as rapacious and grabby as those who work for the public good. They don't want mere millions or billions of dollars to satisfy personal avarice. They seek the trillions of dollars necessary to make life on earth better for everyone. The World Bank should content itself with private good, from which all good things flow.

CHAPTER 6

The Wealth of Nations, Book 2, Continued: Adam Smith, Un-Motivational Speaker

Besides being a discourse on currency and banking, book 2 of *Wealth* is also an examination of economic planning – and the crying need for less of it. Adam Smith was one of the first and best campaigners in the endless war against governmental attempts to control business and industry. Smith's strategy was to convince the people who guide the world's economies to get lost.

The 13 Habits of Highly (It Is to Be Hoped) Ineffective Government Economic Planners

1. Be vulgar and obvious.

The point of government economic planning is, presumably, to better the condition of those whom the government governs. The trouble comes when economic planners start thinking about what that better condition should be. Easier access to mass transportation? More parks and green spaces? Improved educational opportunities? The governed, Smith declared, already know the answer: 'An augmentation of fortune is the means by which the greater part of men propose and wish to better their condition. It is the means the most vulgar and the most obvious.'[1]

2. Let John Q. Citizen do all the work.

Smith emphasized the 'private frugality and good conduct of individuals' and 'their universal, continual, and uninterrupted effort to better their own condition'. He argued that it was 'this effort, protected by law and allowed by liberty ... which has maintained the progress of England towards opulence and improvement'.[2] But since England 'has never been blessed with a very parsimonious government, ... [it] is the highest impertinence and presumption, therefore, in kings and ministers, to pretend to watch over the economy of private people'.[3]

3. Make the whole government as unproductive as the economic planners are.

Government is supposed to be unproductive. Adam Smith divided labor into two types: 'One sort of labour ... adds to the value of the subject upon which it is bestowed.'[4] Government is the other sort. There's nothing wrong with this. 'The labour,' Smith wrote, 'of some of the most respectable orders in the society is ... unproductive of any value.'[5] He didn't mean their labor *had* no value; he meant it didn't produce any physical item. 'Unproductive' labor doesn't result in the physical things – goods, capital, raw materials – that are needed for the production of other physical things. And it is by physical things that we live. No piece of legislation, however well written, will keep you warm outdoors in the winter. (Although *not* passing some legislation, such as the Kyoto Climate Accord, may.)

'The sovereign, for example,' wrote Smith, 'with all the officers both of justice and war ... the whole army and navy, are unproductive labourers ... The protection, security, and defence of the commonwealth, the effect of their labour this year, will not purchase its protection, security, and defence for the year to come.'[6] In other words government is a service, and it should never be mistaken for a factory that furnishes us with all our jobs, homes, and discount blood pressure pills. Whenever a politician is heard to say that government spending is 'an investment', he should be told to get a job.

Later economists, such as, in the early nineteenth century, J. B. Say, felt that Smith undervalued the economic contributions of services. And he did. The eighteenth century had servants, not a service economy. It was hard for a man of that era to believe that the semi-inebriated footman and the blowsy scullery maid would evolve into, well, the stoned pizza delivery boy and the girl behind the checkout counter with an earring in her tongue.

Smith was trying to make a – probably unnecessary – logical distinction between goods and services. But if Smith undervalued private services, this is more than compensated for by the overvaluation of public services made by 'public servants', past and present. The stuff that government consumes must, ultimately, be provided by the people who make and do stuff. Smith noted that 'unproductive labourers' are 'maintained by the annual produce of the land and labour of the country. This produce, how great so-ever, can never be infinite, but must have certain limits.'[7] And certain limits are precisely what government should have.

4. Keep government spending in check. Let other spending run wild.

'Great nations,' Smith wrote, 'are never impoverished by private, though they sometimes are by public prodigality and misconduct.'[8] The reason for this is that 'the man who borrows in order to spend will soon be ruined, and he who lends to him will generally have occasion to repent of his folly. To borrow or to lend for such a purpose, therefore, is in all cases, where gross usury is out of the question, contrary to the interests of both parties.'[9] But Smith had never heard of credit cards. Looking at my MasterCard bill, gross usury is by no means out of the question.

5. Wreck the balance of trade.

Adam Smith, hearing the same frightened complaints about balance of payments as we hear today, slapped the face of trade deficit hysterics: 'But though so great a quantity of gold and silver [or US Treasury bills, or what have you] is thus sent abroad, we must not imagine that it is sent abroad for nothing, or that its proprietors make a present of it to foreign nations.'[10]

6. Everybody hates lower trade barriers. Lower them anyway.

Broader prosperity requires broader markets. Early in book 1 of *Wealth* Smith wrote, 'As it is the power of exchanging that gives occasion to the division of labour, so the extent of this division must always be limited by the extent of that power, or, in other words, by the extent of the market.'[11]

To give a contemporary instance, Palestinian terrorists use division of labor to make bombs that they are eager to exchange for death and destruction in Israel. But the extent of their power of exchange is limited because Israel is not in the market for being blown up, so the terrorists have to strap the bombs to themselves.

Perhaps, come to think of it, this isn't the happiest example to have given. Although it does show that, as good as international free trade is in the abstract, some very bad things do come across borders. That's why any expectation 'that the freedom of trade should ever be entirely restored' is, as Smith believed, 'absurd'. And Smith himself couldn't resist being a bit of a puritanical scold on the subject of foreign trade: 'Purchasing ... such goods as are likely to be consumed by idle people who produce nothing, such as foreign wines, foreign silks, &c ... promotes prodigality.'[12] Our importation of navel-exposing foreign pants consumed by idle teens probably falls into this category. It's best to stick with Smith's original slap in the face.

7. Human capital – it ain't just PhDs.

In addition to expanded markets, economic growth depends upon labor's use of capital, or 'stock'. At the beginning of book 2 Smith lists different kinds of stock including 'the acquired and useful abilities of all the inhabitants or members of the society'.[13] These are certainly as important to economic development as your savings account, and more important than mine. But in the language of modern economic planning, 'promoting human capital' tends to mean large-scale government intrusions upon the education and training of everyone the government can get ahold of. President Bush calls his intrusion No Child Left Behind. What if the kid deserves to be left behind? What if he deserves a smack on the behind?

Adam Smith was only a tepid advocate of public education. As he went on to explain in book 5 of *Wealth,* he thought that some government subsidy of education was needed so that 'even a common labourer may afford it.'[14] Teachers, however, should be 'partly, but not wholly paid' by the state. 'In modern times, the diligence of public teachers is more or less corrupted by the circumstances, which render them more or less independent of their success and reputation,'[15] wrote Smith, making his modern times sound like ours. And Smith believed that certain very prestigious institutions of higher learning were teaching 'a mere useless and pedantic heap of sophistry and nonsense'.[16] Was UC Berkeley even around back then?

The educational programs of modern governments aim at turning out droves of eminent specialists. No doubt specialists are useful to division of labor. But Smith meant us to appreciate something that is more ordinary and (even with marginal utility factored in) more valuable than a specialist. By categorizing 'useful abilities' as capital, Smith was returning to a principle put forth in the consideration of the division of labor in book 1. Every man should be given the respect accorded to an eminent specialist, even 'the common ploughman, ... regarded as the pattern of stupidity and ignorance'.[17] Every man is a specialist in what he needs and wants. And the most stupid and ignorant man is more than that. 'No apprenticeship has ever been thought necessary to qualify for husbandry,'[18] Smith wrote. (Or, as we'd put it – no Rhodes Scholarship, postgraduate degree, or MacArthur genius grant is required to hoe cabbage.) And yet, Smith pointed out, countless highly specialized books have been written about agriculture. 'And from all those volumes we shall in vain attempt to collect that knowledge of its various and complicated operations, which is commonly possessed even by the common farmer; how contemptuously soever the very contemptible authors of some of them may sometimes affect to speak of him.'[19]

Just a few years ago the 'common ploughman' of China was thought to possess no human capital at all. Today he's reckoned to be the most potent economic force in the world. It's not because a billion Chinese peasants got MBAs.

In 1944 Friedrich A. Hayek published *The Road to Serfdom*, history's second most important book about economics. Hayek's denunciation of economic planning was dedicated 'To socialists of all parties'. In his chapter titled 'The "Inevitability" of Planning', he wrote that 'there could hardly be a more unbearable – and more irrational – world than one in which the most eminent specialists in each field were allowed to proceed unchecked with the realization of their ideals.'[20]

Adam Smith and Friedrich Hayek warned us about the marvelous South Korean educational system and allowing Woo Suk Hwang to proceed unchecked with the bogus cloning of human embryonic stem cells.

8. Buy retail.

Adam Smith was one of the few deep thinkers – wives excepted – to ever come to the defense of retailing. 'If,' he wrote, 'there was no such trade as a butcher, for example, every man would be obliged to purchase a whole ox or a whole sheep at a time. This would generally be inconvenient to the rich, and much more so to the poor.'[21] And even a two-lawyer family with a Sub-Zero freezer might have quite a time getting an ox in there.

And yet, distaste for retailing is nearly universal. There is the aristocratic horror of being in trade (other than the military trade of butchering humans). And there is the bourgeois horror experienced by those who got caught being in trade by the likes of Stalin. 'Mom and pop stores' and the 'corner shop' are sometimes extolled, but the places where everyone buys everything never are. In rural New England where I live, the conservative preservationist kooks, who want every 7-Eleven replaced with a collapsing barn, join amiably with the liberal back-to-nature dopes, who think highway potholes should be protected as wetland resources. Together they have ensured that it's an hour's drive to the nearest Wal-Mart. 'The prejudices of some political writers against shopkeepers and tradesmen, are altogether without foundation,' Smith wrote. 'They can never be multiplied so as to hurt the publick, though they may so as to hurt one another.' The wise enemy of Wal-Mart wants one right in town – with a Target next door.

9. Modern life is stressful, overscheduled, and job-obsessed – keep it that way.

Don't fall into the UN Universal Declaration of Human Rights trap, where everyone is declared to have 'the right to rest and leisure'. Look where it's gotten the UN. 'Our ancestors,' Smith wrote, 'were idle for a want of a sufficient encouragement to industry. It is better, says the proverb, to play for nothing, than to work for nothing.'[22] What our ancestors played was 'hunt the witch' and 'kill the Jews' and 'send the kids on the Children's Crusade'.

The life of earning has merits that the life of spending what others have earned lacks. As pointless as existence in the workplace cubicle seems, it's not as pointless as hanging out at the mall. To illustrate this tenet Smith compares cities where the business is government with cities where the business is business. 'In those towns which are principally supported by the constant or occasional residence of a court [read George Bush or Tony Blair], and in which the inferior ranks of people are chiefly maintained by the spending of revenue, they are in general idle, dissolute, and poor.'[23] Idle and dissolute in London. Poor in Washington, DC. By contrast, 'In mercantile and manufacturing towns, where the inferior ranks of people are chiefly maintained by the employment of capital, they are in general industrious, sober, and thriving.'[24] Of course nowadays that would be in Guangzhou.

10. *Don't put your money in a safe place.*

And if you can't think of anything better to do with your money, spend it. Smith wrote that 'every man of common understanding will endeavour to employ whatever stock he can command, in procuring either present enjoyment or future profit.'[25] Indeed, he wrote, 'A man must be perfectly crazy who, where there is tolerable security, does not employ all the stock which he commands, whether it be his own or borrowed of other people.'[26] But, continued Smith, 'In those unfortunate countries ... where men are continually afraid of the violence of their superiors, they frequently bury and conceal a great part of their stock.'[27]

The survivalist madly provisioning his off-the-grid compound, the hapless retiree buying gold advertised on TV, the lonely recluse hoarding string, aluminum foil, and pre-1965 silver dimes – they are not as crazy as the political and economic systems that make them think they need to do this. And 'afraid of the violence of their superiors' is not too strong a phrase for people who've been through an IRS audit.

11. *Get all confused about globalization.*

The complexity of economics can be calculated mathematically. Write out the algebraic equation that is the human heart and multiply each unknown by the population of the world. In his commentary on farmers Adam Smith proved, whether he meant to or not, that economics is unknowable. What rednecks do in the barn is deeply recondite (and who knows what else). The hopeless perplexity of economics is the best hope of keeping us humble when we are perplexed by it. If we think we have a theory that untangles the economic skein, we are kittens with a ball of yarn – killer kittens if we want to tie up others with that yarn and drown them in the well of idealism.

The danger of trying to deduce specific economic policy from general economic theory is something else that Adam Smith proved, in a manner that humbled himself. The last dozen or so pages of book 2 concern what we would call globalization. The man who created modern economics was as muddled as any modern on the subject.

Smith began with a Khmer Rouge praise of agriculture: 'Of all the ways in which a capital can be employed, it is by far the most advantageous to the society.'[28] He followed this with a misunderstanding of the international capital market: 'The capital of the manufacturer must no doubt reside where the manufacture is carried on.'[29] Smith partially corrected that misunderstanding in the first sentence of the next paragraph: 'Whether the merchant whose capital exports the surplus produce of any society be a native or a foreigner, is of very little importance.'[30] And in the paragraph after that Smith managed to both misunderstand and not misunderstand at the same time: 'It is of more consequence that the capital of the manufacturer should reside within the country ... It may, however, be very useful to the country, though it should not reside within it.'[31]

Smith emerged from his bewilderment about domestic and international capital long enough to expose the folly of economic planners in developing countries who think self-sufficiency in agriculture, manufacturing, and transportation is the way to prosperity: 'To attempt, however, prematurely and with an insufficient capital, to do all the three, is certainly not the shortest way.'[32] But Smith didn't know that the United States would soon provide a contrary example. 'Were the Americans,' Smith wrote, 'to stop the importation of European manufactures, and, by thus giving a monopoly to such of their own countrymen as could manufacture the like goods ... they would retard instead of accelerating the further increase in the value of their annual produce.'[33]

For the following 150 years America would impose tariffs on foreign manufactured goods at rates ranging from damn high to higher. Of course America would become the exception that proved the rule by making use of a vast internal free market. Also, it's scarier to think that Smith was right about the effects of American protectionism than to think that he was wrong. Consider an America that had gotten as rich in the 1850s as it is now – with nothing to spend the money on but more slaves and larger hoop skirts, horse whips, and pistols.

Having rendered the utilization and flow of capital incomprehensible and left us confused about developing economies, Smith went on to immerse himself in obscurities concerning rate of return on investment: 'But the returns of the foreign trade of consumption are very seldom so quick as those of the home-trade.'[34] By emphasizing the value of quick profit Smith argued against his own argument in favor of agriculture. Making money by farming is, exactly, like watching grass grow. Smith was also touching upon the theory of 'velocity of money', which would be fully stated by John Maynard Keynes in the 1930s and which no one has ever understood, Keynes included.

Smith finished his section on globalization with an observation about human ingenuity in the exercise of market freedoms that rendered everything he'd just written about capital meaningless: 'We see every day the most splendid fortunes that have been acquired in the course of a single life by trade and manufactures, frequently from a very small capital, sometimes from no capital.'[35]

12. Ignore the experts.

Smith wrote, 'Five years have seldom passed away in which some book or pamphlet has not been published ... pretending to demonstrate that the wealth of the nation was fast declining.'[36]

13. Especially, ignore the economists.

Knowing something about economics does not alter the fact that economics is unknowable. Economists cannot predict the future any better than Jennifer Aniston and Donald Rumsfeld could predict Brad Pitt and Iraq.

Adam Smith arguably knew almost everything that could be known about economics in the late eighteenth century, but he failed to foresee the importance of the 'joint stock company' or corporation. Modern capitalism's mentor didn't believe that the institution central to modern capitalism could work. Smith described corporations as having 'an immense capital divided among an immense number of proprietors'[37] and wrote, 'It was naturally to be expected, therefore, that folly, negligence, and profusion should prevail in the whole management of their affairs.'[38] Of course, as it turns out, Smith was right oftener than investors in common stock would like.

More tellingly, Smith failed to predict the Industrial Revolution. Not only did Smith fail to predict the Industrial Revolution, he did so while being friends with the inventor of the steam engine, James Watt. Smith helped Watt find workspace at Glasgow University after the local ironmongers guild (doing all it could to prove, by negative example, Smith's thesis on market freedoms) refused to let Watt set up shop in town. Smith socialized with Watt at meetings of the Glasgow Dining Club, and, while writing *The Wealth of Nations,* invested in a machine for industrial duplication that Watt had developed. Plus Smith fully appreciated the genius of Watt. In an early draft of *Wealth,* Smith wrote, 'It was a real philosopher only who could invent the fire engine.'[39] (Giving that name to a device for steam propulsion makes us think of men with helmets, hoses, and dalmatians trying to take the train to our house when the roof is ablaze. But, in fairness, it's an accurate term.)

Adam Smith didn't forecast the Industrial Revolution for the simple reason that he thought it had already happened. Smith held that there were three ways to increase the 'annual produce', the GDP, of a nation. Population could grow, which doesn't do much for GDP per capita. Division of labor could advance, which has its obvious limits. (That is, I could write verbs and nouns, subcontract adverbs and adjectives, and get a minimum wage worker to insert prepositions and conjunctions.) The third way to increase GDP was 'some addition and improvement to those machines and instruments which facilitate and abridge labour'.[40] Smith felt that this last method was so self-evidently the most important that he didn't bother to expound upon it. In the first chapter of the first book of *Wealth* he wrote that 'every body must be sensible how much labour is facilitated and abridged by the application of proper machinery. It is unnecessary to give any example.'[41]

What Smith guessed wrong about was not the qualitative nature of the Industrial Revolution but the huge, world-shattering quantity of the thing. Smith opposed the predictive pretensions of economic planning and proved himself right with his own failure as an economic fortune-teller.

The fact that Smith was missing some letters from his Ouija board is to be remembered when we hear experts pontificate on the Computer Revolution. Its results may turn out to be a dozen times greater than we expect (a dozen being about the number by which western European GDP per capita was multiplied between the 1820s and the 1990s). Or its results may be nearly over and done with, and the Computer Revolution may be remembered mostly as a period during which individuals wearing unfashionable eyeglasses, relaxed-fit Levis, and GOOGLE ME T-shirts were briefly thought dateworthy.

CHAPTER 7

The Wealth of Nations, Book 3 'Of the different Progress of Opulence in different Nations' and How We Have the Stupidity of the Powerful to Thank for It

The first two books of *The Wealth of Nations* are Adam Smith's creed of economic progress. Smith placed his faith not in the belief that man is good or that God is great but in the logic of common sense. We are required to care for ourselves. We act upon this requirement. Our actions are demonstrably beneficial to others. The economy progresses, QED. Or it would, Smith wrote, 'if human institutions had never thwarted those natural inclinations'.[1]

Book 3 of *Wealth* is Smith's examination of institutions that thwart and how their unthwarting is achieved. The title is misleading. Smith compares opulence at different times, rather than different places, in a capsule economic history of western

Europe from the fall of the Roman Empire until the end of feudalism. This summary, the gist of which is little more than thirty pages long, contains perhaps the most brilliant (and definitely the most succinct) of all Smith's analyses.

His delineation of causes and effects is especially brilliant for us, the lucky inheritors of western European economic progress. Luck is always rare, but having access to the mechanism by which luck is produced is almost unheard of. To read book 3 is to get a rabbit's foot that hops around on a *Wall Street Journal* page picking hot stocks.

What happened to the Roman provinces of Europe in the fifth century AD can be compared to an invasion of those aldermen's wives whom Smith described in *The Theory of Moral Sentiments*. The 'great object' of the barbarians was, precisely, 'place … the cause of all the tumult and bustle, all the rapine and injustice'.[2]

Smith wrote that the 'rapine and violence which the barbarians exercised' left western Europe 'sunk into the lowest state of poverty'.[3] Commerce was destroyed, towns were deserted, fields were left uncultivated. But although the rule of law and the legal title to property that goes with it were destroyed, the result was not 'Imagine no possessions / I wonder if you can.' Nothing in the ruined Roman Empire was, Smith reminded us, 'left without a proprietor'.[4] A vacuum of power is not filled with pop idol musings, nor with anarcho-syndicalists either. A vacuum of power is filled with more and worse power. The petty tribal chieftains who stole western

Europe made Mikhail Bakunin look as tame and middle class as an alderman's wife's husband.

Barbarian leaders did not grab land in order to become rich. They were rich. Shopping is easy and convenient when you do it with a large band of armed men. Albeit there wasn't much to shop for in the Dark Ages. What the barbarian proprietors did with the produce of their domains was give it away.

They didn't do this because they were generous. They did it because they were greedy for yet more power. 'A great proprietor,' Smith wrote, 'having nothing for which he can exchange the greater part of the produce of his lands ... consumes the whole in rustic hospitality at home.'[5] This did not mean jesters and jousts and throwing chicken bones on the floor at the Medieval Times restaurant chain. It meant feeding thugs. The more thugs a chieftain could feed, the more powerful he was. Smith pointed out that in the time of William Rufus, son of William the Conqueror, Westminster Hall was not a seat of Parliament; it was a dining room. 'Land was considered as the means, not of subsistence merely,' wrote Smith, 'but of power and protection ...[6] Authority ... flowed from the state of property.'[7]

That property equals power was a concept leftists were quick to seize upon. But it was capitalism that expanded the definition of property and weakened the equation. Power used to rest in a limited commodity. There was a finite amount of power because there was a finite amount of land. Any power that I could get was power I took from you when

I stole your backyard. By turning power into money instead of real estate, capitalism made power infinite and began the process of separating economic power from the power to dominate fellow humans: 'A person who either acquires, or succeeds to a great fortune, does not necessarily acquire or succeed to any political power.'[8] It is the socialists who would be the new feudal overlords, the fortressed thugs. They would return the source of power to the limited commodity that is politics. Any power that I can get is power I take from you when I steal an election.

Feudalism is now a bandy-about word that we use to disparage any type of authority that we don't particularly like. But Adam Smith had a politically informed animus against feudalism. When he was a young man, studying at Oxford's Balliol College, the feudal Highland clans rose in the Jacobite Rebellion of 1745. Then, as now, the personal was political. The English students at Balliol were both Jacobite and bigoted against Scots. Smith was a Scot and an anti-Jacobite.

Not only were Smith's feelings hurt at school, the Highlanders threatened his hometown of Kirkcaldy and extorted money from its citizens, among whom was Smith's mother. Glasgow, where Smith had gone to the university, was overrun. And Smith's friend, the dramatist John Home, led a band of student volunteers in a vain attempt to keep the invaders out of Edinburgh.

Another friend of Smith's, the liberal Presbyterian minister Alexander Carlyle, called the Highlanders who occupied Edinburgh 'short and dirty, and of a contemptible appearance'.[9]

It is a description that can be used for the entire feudal nobility of western Europe from Alaric to the time when aristocrats started marrying American movie stars. The more so if we apply 'short' to tempers and attention spans, 'dirty' to morals, and 'contemptible appearance' to the fact that the feudal nobility appeared in western Europe at all.

Smith detested the customs of primogeniture and entail that kept feudal estates in one piece. The nobles forbade themselves to sell or give away any land, willing it all to a single heir. They did so, Smith wrote, 'upon the most absurd of all suppositions ... that every successive generation of men have not an equal right to the earth, and to all that it possesses'.[10] The restrictions on land conveyance allowed the nobility to make sure that everyone's livelihood depended on them, the welfare state politicians of their day.

There was another reason that self-sufficiency of ordinary people on small freeholds had to be prevented. Yeomen were better farmers than jerks in armor. 'It seldom happens,' Smith wrote, 'that a great proprietor is a great improver.'[11] Primogeniture and entail were needed to prevent the peasants from getting the economic upper hand. The ruling class, Smith noted, was too busy to be productive. 'In the disorderly times which gave birth to those barbarous institutions, the great proprietor was sufficiently employed in defending his own territories, or in extending his jurisdiction.'[12] And when the ruling class wasn't too busy, it was incompetent. 'To improve land with profit,' Smith wrote, 'requires an exact attention to small savings and small gains, of which a man born to a great fortune ... is very seldom capable.'[13] Let the villains own land and pretty soon Mary Dairymaid with her muddy plot and five cows is able to feed more thugs than Charlemagne.

Smith was outraged 'that the property of the present generation should be restrained and regulated according to the fancy of those who died perhaps five hundred years ago'.[14] It was an outrage that persisted with the landed gentry of Smith's time. And it persists today when we are told by ecological activists that we don't really 'own' land because 'it belongs to future generations' – the property of the present generation to be restrained and regulated according to the fancy of those who haven't been born yet. Maybe Jane Austen, in *Pride and Prejudice,* meant silly Mrs Bennet to speak unintended wisdom: 'There is no knowing how estates will go when once they come to be entailed.'[15]

How life itself went on the estates of the feudal era is easy to imagine – or see, if you take an 'adventure tour' to certain parts of Africa, Asia, and Latin America. In the Dark Ages everyone was a child laborer in a Guatemalan sneaker factory (without the sneakers). 'They were,' Smith wrote, 'all or almost all slaves.'[16] Slaves don't have private property rights. But feudal slaves didn't even have the right to be the private property of someone else. 'They were,' Smith wrote, 'supposed to belong more directly to the land than to their masters.'[17] Masters, at least, would have some selfish interest in the well-being of their slaves. The feudal nobility had none. As a result the nobility's land never yielded much. 'If great improvements are seldom to be expected from great proprietors,' Smith continued, 'they are least of all to be expected when they employ slaves for their workmen.'[18]

Here Smith took an opportunity to make his economic argument against slavery: 'The experience of all ages and nations, I believe, demonstrates that the work done by slaves, though it appears to cost only their maintenance, is in the end the dearest of any. A person who can acquire no property, can have no other interest but to eat as much, and to labour as little as possible.'[19] This wouldn't be much of a slogan for abolitionists. But cold calculation has done more for mankind than William Wilberforce, Harriet Beecher Stowe, or John Brown.

Feudal serfs may have been inclined to sit around eating (when there was anything to eat), but they weren't fools. They took advantage of the nobility's hectic rapine and violence schedule to keep a bit of trade going on their own account. Besides, some trade is necessary to even the most squalid and basic existence.

Unable to stop trade, the nobility instituted a protection racket. 'In those days,' Smith wrote, 'protection was seldom granted without a valuable consideration.'[20] Or in these days either. Thus, 'taxes used to be levied upon the persons and goods of travellers.'[21] The serfs were shaken down when they crossed a nobleman's land, went over his bridge, carried a load of goods to a market, or set up a trading booth. According to Smith the English names for these exactions were 'passage, pontage, lastage, and stallage',[22] an excellent law firm by the sound of it.

With so many thugs to feed, the nobility was always broke. It wasn't long before canny serfs figured out that noblemen liked a lump sum payment better than an unpredictable take from the random skinning of wayfarers. And the serfs were probably more clever than the nobles at computing the advantage of this flat tax. They hadn't had their counting fingers cut off in sword fights.

The traders who made set payments to someone in authority, and therefore were liberated from minor tariffs and imposts, were known as 'free-traders' or, since they traded in market towns, 'free-burghers'. The market towns grew until there were enough burghers to band together – not to defy the nobles but to bribe them more efficiently. The burghers formed themselves into corporations. The corporation made a guarantee to the feudal overlord that he would receive the tribute due from each free-trader, all at once, in an even larger lump sum (minus handling fees, of course). And the corporation would take care of all the fuss and bother of collecting the money. This left the feudal overlords with more time for fighting.

By undertaking to levy their own taxes on themselves, the burghers escaped visits from bailiffs collecting payoffs and from other feudal interferences. With money and guile, Smith argued, the burghers began to gain a measure of control over their own affairs, 'that they might give away their own daughters in marriage, that their children should succeed to them, and that they might dispose of their own effects by will ... The principle attributes of villanage and slavery being thus taken away from them, they now … became really free in our present sense of the word Freedom.'[23]

It turns out that wealthy corporations, rather than perverting private property rights, are a source of them. And, although freedom may be an inherent human right, we know where we really got our freedom. We bought it.

As for the price that we paid, it was a steal. The liberties that the burghers purchased from the feudal rulers were almost universally granted, not for a percentage of free-trader business, but for a fixed annual price in gold. The lordly descendants of short, dirty barbarians didn't understand economic growth or inflation. They didn't understand anything but violence. One can almost hear Adam Smith's satisfaction:

> But it must seem extraordinary that the sovereigns of all the different countries of Europe, should have exchanged in this manner for a rent certain, never more to be augmented, that branch of their revenue, which was, perhaps, of all others the most likely to be improved by the natural course of things, without either expence or attention of their own.[24]

A good head for business is a middle-class invention. The ancient Greeks and Romans, for all their genius, didn't have it. Otherwise they would have abandoned slave labor with its health benefit and pension plan burdens. They would have freed the slaves, turned them into customers, and outsourced the unskilled jobs to Sogdiana and Gaul. The medieval burghers, besides becoming really free, became really smart in our present sense of the word. 'The habits,' Smith wrote, 'of order, œconomy and attention, to which mercantile business naturally forms a merchant, render him much fitter to execute, with profit and success, any project of improvement.'[25]

Good government is another middle-class invention. Political savvy was necessary to the survival of the towns. The burghers were geese laying golden eggs for the feudal powers, and we know how that story ended. To keep themselves from being figuratively – and perhaps literally – gutted, the townsmen played the feudal powers against each other.

Adam Smith didn't allow himself to be lured into the historical thicket of how kingships arose and nation-states coalesced. But the invading barbarians had been impressed by the grand, sweeping Roman concept of *emperor*. The most powerful of the feudal nobles were always professing suzerainty over lesser lords and claiming to be king of this or that.

'The lords despised the burghers,' Smith wrote, 'whom they considered ... a parcel of emancipated slaves ... The burghers naturally hated and feared the lords. The king hated and feared them too; but ... he had no reason either to hate or fear the burghers.'[26] Who could hate a helpless source of revenue? Meanwhile the king's bullies were usually farther away than the local landlord's bullies, so the burghers liked the king better. 'Mutual interest ... disposed them to support the king, and the king to support them against the lords.'[27] (And there remains an affinity between prosperous city dwellers and strong central government. This is evident in the political opinions of urban elites. Likewise, the tradition of helplessness still forms urban elite opinions about gun control.)

In order for the burghers to operate with political savvy they had to have their own politics in hand. Factious towns couldn't manage the balance of king against nobles and would fall prey to both. 'Commerce and manufactures,' Smith wrote, 'gradually introduced order and good government, and with them, the liberty and security of individuals, among the inhabitants of the country, who had before lived almost in a continual state of war with their neighbours, and of servile dependency upon their superiors.'[28]

Leftist critics of free markets assume that there is a fraudulent aspect to capitalism. They're right. We tricked the feudal powers into setting us free, and we remained free by continuing to bamboozle them. We used chicanery and sharp dealing to found our cities, become rich bourgeoisie, and supply ourselves with creature comforts. We left the barbarian aristocracy in their drafty castles throwing chicken bones on the floor.

And we were by no means finished with cheating the nobility. We did the worst that can be done to fools; we gave them what they wanted. The towns imported luxury goods and developed arts and crafts. Among these products the nobles discovered things that they'd rather spend their money on than feeding thugs. Feast budgets were trimmed. Barbarian hospitality was curtailed.

Adam Smith argued that the inclination of the feudal overlords to be selfish was so strong that it overwhelmed their instinct for self-preservation:

> All for ourselves, and nothing for other people, seems,
> in every age of the world, to have been the vile maxim of
> the masters of mankind. As soon, therefore, as they could
> find a method of consuming the whole value of their rents
> themselves, they had no disposition to share them with any
> other persons. For a pair of diamond buckles perhaps, or for
> something as frivolous and useless, they exchanged ... the
> price of the maintenance of a thousand men for a year, and
> with it the whole weight and authority which it could give
> them. The buckles, however, were to be all their own, and
> no other human creature was to have any share of them;
> whereas in the more ancient method of expence they must
> have shared with at least a thousand people ... and thus,
> for the gratification of the most childish, the meanest and
> the most sordid of all vanities, they gradually bartered their
> whole power and authority.[29]

Never complain that the people in power are stupid. It is their best trait. In recent years we've seen a variety of powerful figures barter their authority for the gratification of childish vanities. Perhaps the Saudi royal family will be next to suffer the fate that Adam Smith described:

> Having sold their birth-right, not like Esau for a mess of
> pottage in time of hunger and necessity, but in the wan-
> tonness of plenty, for trinkets and baubles, fitter to be the
> play-things of children than the serious pursuits of men,

they became as insignificant as any substantial burgher or tradesman in a city.[30]

The destruction of feudal oppression, the establishment of the principle of self-government, and the creation of 'freedom in our present sense of the word Freedom' – it was all a swindle. There were no passionate orations by visionary idealists. No heroes led the masses in throwing off their chains. No one was martyred for the cause. 'A revolution of the greatest importance to the public happiness,' wrote Smith, 'was in this manner brought about by two different orders of people, who had not the least intention to serve the public.'[31]

The Wealth of Nations, Book 4 'Of Systems of Political Economy' Adam Smith Tackles the Chinese Trade Menace

If a single practical reason for reading *The Wealth of Nations* had to be given, it could be stated in three words, 'global free trade'. Or, since there's a particular example of global free trade that alarms us more than any other, one word will suffice: China.

Thinking about China seems to induce intellectual Chinese fire drills and cause otherwise clear-thinking individuals to fuddle themselves with calculations – harder than Chinese arithmetic – about what this, that, or the other thing has to do with the price of tea in you-know-where. We have been amazed and perplexed by China since *The Travels of Marco Polo*. It's so big, so populous, so ... Chinese. And until the end of the thirteenth century we didn't even realize it was there.

Of course we'd been trading with China, whether we knew it or not, since the time of the Roman Empire. But trade with

China remains a source of surprise and shock. It seems the Chinese are selling everything to us. And we are selling hardly anything to the Chinese. China is growing ferociously rich. And what will become of us?

Panicky articles about balance of trade clutter the *New York Times* and other broadsheets. In 2005 I began tearing these items out of the papers and stuffing them into my pockets until I looked like something that was going to be burned in effigy (a fate not always undeserved by amateurs who write about economics).

The United States imports a great deal more than it exports, due in large part to the China trade. At my house I see a MADE IN CHINA label on everything but the kids and the dogs. And I'm not sure about the kids. They have brown eyes and small noses.

In June 2005, the US quarterly trade deficit reached $195 billion. The *New York Times* claimed that 'the news reignited worries that the economy cannot sustain the growing level of global debt.' Importing all of our goods except for golden retrievers means American money must be sent overseas to pay the bills. Money is a promissory note. American IOUs are piling up. The *Times* article pointed out that 'the United States borrows, in essence, $2.1 billion every day to keep the economy afloat.'

Never mind that an international 'current account deficit' is not comparable to a private debt. Hu Jintao is not going to show up at my door threatening to repossess my DVD player because he has a fifty-dollar bill that I owe on.

This fact did not stop the *New York Times* from finding pan-ickers to quote. North Dakota Senator Byron Dorgan said that the deficit was reaching 'dangerous levels that are hurting this country's future'. And Maryland Congressman Benjamin L. Cardin said (using the synonym for 'future' that sets off the baloney alert), 'The deficit raises serious questions about our ability to control our destiny.'

A *New York Times Magazine* article, also in June 2005, pro-claimed that, 'A low-level panic about the debt crisis, and its possible effect on the American economy, is gathering strength.' Former Federal Reserve Chairman Paul Volcker was quoted: 'Altogether, the circumstances seem to me as dangerous and intractable as any I can remember.' Volcker became chairman of the Federal Reserve during the woeful Carter administra-tion, so that's a strong statement. Although maybe Volcker was forgetting how dangerous and intractable Rosalynn Carter could be.

In a *Washington Post* op-ed piece in February 2005, senior foreign correspondent Jim Hoagland wrote, 'A handful of Asian countries headed by China ... hold nearly 70 percent of the world's foreign exchange reserves ... This is the new global balance of terror: China ... could bring the U.S. economy to its knees by massively selling off the dollar.'

Pundits were upset about what was happening with Ameri-can money, and they were upset about what was happening with Chinese money, too. It seems that the Chinese have been insisting that their money, the yuan, is worth much less than whatever the fashionable price theory of the moment says it's really, truly worth. 'Critics of China,' noted the *New York Times* (itself being a significant one), 'charge that the yuan is badly undervalued ... giving Chinese manufacturers an unfair competitive advantage.'

A *Times* op-ed piece written by Senators Charles Schumer and Lindsey Graham (or, rather, written by some underpaid junior staffers who majored in the vagaries of Poli Sci) began: 'Dismayed by China's failure to play fair on free trade, we have offered legislation to impose a tariff on Chinese exports to the United States if Beijing continues to keep the value of its currency, the yuan, artificially low compared with the dollar.'

In the matter of free trade, the other country's currency can't *be* too low. It's like going to a Los Angeles real estate agent and being told, 'There's a house in Beverly Hills. The price is five million dollars. But the sellers will accept five million Mexican pesos.'

Even a cursory read of *The Wealth of Nations* would calm Schumer, Graham, Hoagland, and the rest of them.

Or maybe it wouldn't. These men are members of the American establishment. And Adam Smith was an anti-establishment activist – a threat to their power and privilege. Smith was trying to better the economic condition of ordinary people. This is a subversive enterprise, as *Wealth*'s book 3 on the destruction of feudalism showed. And an important part of Smith's subversion was his attempt to refute the mercantilist thinking of his time (and of the *Times*, if he could have seen into the future).

In book 4 of *Wealth*, Smith devotes as much space to squelching the mercantilists as he devotes, in book 1, to setting forth his basic principles of unfettered division of labor and freedom of trade. His attack on the mercantile establishment caused Smith to revisit certain of his earlier arguments. He reapplied logic to such subjects as government subsidies for domestic industry: 'the trade which cannot be carried on but by means of a bounty being necessarily a losing trade.'[1] And he offered additional proofs that the worth of money is subjective, in case some eighteenth-century *New York Times* editorial board didn't get it the first time. Smith tried to make these reiterations worthwhile for his more astute readers. Concerning currency valuations, Smith offered this anecdote:

> For some time after the discovery of America, the first enquiry of the Spaniards ... used to be, if there was any gold or silver to be found in the neighbourhood? ... Plano Carpino, a monk sent as ambassador from the king of France to one of the sons of the famous Gengis Khan, says that the Tartars used frequently to ask him, if there was plenty of sheep and oxen in the kingdom of France? Their enquiry had the same object with that of the Spaniards. They wanted to know if the country was rich enough to be worth the conquering. Among the Tartars ... cattle are the instruments of commerce and the measures of value. Wealth, therefore, according to them, consisted in cattle, as according to the Spaniards it consisted in gold and silver. Of the two, the Tartar notion, perhaps, was the nearest to the truth.[2]

The mercantilists could never quite bring themselves to believe that the cows in their pockets weren't the real measure of their wealth. They could not see that, as Smith put it, 'Goods can serve many other purposes besides purchasing money, but money can serve no other purpose besides purchasing goods.'[3]

Money going out must be some sort of problem no matter how many high-quality, low-priced consumer electronic goods are coming in. 'That foreign trade enriched the country, experience demonstrated,' Smith wrote, 'but how, or in what manner, none of them well knew.'[4]

Mercantilists believed that a positive balance of trade, with its current account surplus, was something to be sought – or better, per Senators Schumer and Graham – legislated. Would that one could say Smith triumphed in this debate. There are many pleasant things to read in book 4 of *Wealth*, but it would be more pleasant to tell you to skip it, that Smith is beating a dead horse. However, right now in America it's *Night of the Living Dead Horses*.

'There is no commercial country in Europe of which the approaching ruin has not frequently been foretold … from an unfavourable balance of trade,'[5] Smith wrote, making the news in the *New York Times* and the *Washington Post* very old news indeed. 'Nothing,' Smith wrote, 'can be more absurd than this whole doctrine of the balance of trade.'[6] As Smith had already made clear, every freely conducted trade is balanced by definition. The definition doesn't change because one trader gets an iPod and the other gets an IOU.

Let us concede, for argument's sake, that incurring large debts to get tiny iPods is bad. But doing something about it is worse. Imposing government restrictions on trade means giving up our freedom. We surrender our decision-making skill to, in Smith's words, 'the skill of that insidious and crafty animal, vulgarly called a statesman or politician, whose councils are directed by the momentary fluctuations of affairs'.[7] And of those who are vulgarly so called, Smith wrote:

> The statesman, who should attempt to direct private
> people in what manner they ought to employ their capitals,
> would ... assume an authority which could safely be trusted,
> not only to no single person, but to no council or senate
> whatever, and which would nowhere be so dangerous as in
> the hands of a man who had folly and presumption enough
> to fancy himself fit to exercise it.[8]

Furthermore, Smith argued, this insidious and crafty animal of a Schumer or Graham is a pig oppressor as well:

> To prohibit a great people ... from making all that they can
> of every part of their own produce, or from employing their
> stock and industry in the way that they judge most advan-
> tageous to themselves, is a manifest violation of the most
> sacred rights of mankind.[9]

If, at the moment, the Chinese are the 'great people', so what? Adam Smith foresaw China's industrial capacity (even if he didn't foresee the Industrial Revolution): 'By a more extensive navigation, the Chinese would naturally learn the art of using and constructing themselves all the different machines made use of in other countries.'[10] But in Smith's day the problem was their deep thinkers, not ours. 'The Chinese,' Smith wrote, 'have little respect for foreign trade. Your beggarly commerce! was the language in which the Mandarins of Peking used to talk to Mr. de Lange, the Russian envoy.'[11] (Apparently they convinced him. Russia's commerce is still beggarly in everything except oil, gas, and purloined nuclear warheads.)

Smith disdained trade retaliation: 'Those workmen ... who suffered by our neighbours' prohibition will not be benefited by ours. On the contrary, they and almost all the other classes of our citizens will thereby be obliged to pay dearer than before for certain goods.'[12]

And Smith gave the lie to claims that tariffs protect working stiffs: 'To lay a new tax upon them ... and because they already pay too dear for the necessaries of life, to make them likewise pay too dear for the greater part of other commodities, is certainly a most absurd way of making amends.'[13]

As for all our money going overseas, Smith had shown in book 2 of *Wealth* why this doesn't harm an economy: 'we must not imagine that it is sent abroad for nothing.'[14] And Smith was referring to gold bullion. Gold always has *some* value, at least on wedding anniversaries if you want a quiet life. The American money that the Chinese are getting is fiat currency that could turn into wastepaper at any time. Presents of wastepaper aren't recommended, even on first, or 'paper', anniversaries.

By holding dollars and dollar-denominated securities, China is buying our debt. Smith had declared, 'A man must be perfectly crazy who ... does not employ all the stock which he commands, whether it be his own or borrowed.' If Americans think they're using all the capital they can get their hands on 'in the way that they judge most advantageous to themselves', they'd be crazy not to be in debt.

The Chinese are obviously confident that American money isn't going to become trash. And the Chinese are confident that Americans are making good use of capital, or they wouldn't be loaning it to us. Indeed, the whole world seems to be confident in America, more confident than it is in China. There's no rush to accumulate Chinese debt. Smith Barney isn't urging you to buy yuan.

Everyone's confident in America except America's opinion-makers. They're worried about ... Actually, I can't tell from the panicky newspaper clippings what, exactly, it is that they're worried about.

If the dollar stays valuable, we'll keep having this terrible trade deficit. But if the dollar turns into what you train puppies on, the Chinese may want something more substantive in return for what they send us. We may have to give them a stealth fighter to get a new cell phone.

Adam Smith, were he alive, would have us consider the parable of Japan in the 1980s. The Japanese kept giving us radios, TVs, stereos, and cars, and we kept giving them money. The Japanese didn't want anything America made except Michael Jackson audio cassettes, and we didn't even make the valuable part – the cassette part – of those. So the Japanese decided to buy America itself. They bought office complexes, golf courses, and hotels. The Japanese bid up the price of American real estate until the bubble did what bubbles do. By the 1990s America had all the radios, TVs, stereos, and cars, and all the office complexes, golf courses, and hotels, and all the money, too.

Maybe the Chinese will be more successful than the Japanese in their attempt to make us poor by giving us things. But we are free to refuse the offer. The Chinese have no way to coerce us into trade. They haven't fought a war with us, the way the British fought the Opium Wars with them, to force us to accept their products on their terms. (Although *someone* seems to have fought an Opium War with us, to judge by what goes on in American slums.)

War, Smith pointed out, was the mercantilists' best excuse for curtailing imports and limiting foreign debt. A current account deficit may be economically meaningless, 'but it is otherwise, they think,' wrote Smith, 'with countries . . . which are obliged to carry on foreign wars, and to maintain fleets and armies in distant countries. This, they say, cannot be done, but by sending abroad money to pay them with; and a nation cannot send much money abroad, unless it has a good deal at home.'[15]

The mercantilist policy was 'restraints upon importation, and encouragements to exportation'.[16] But if we implement this policy, then we're trying to do to our own nation in peacetime what we try to do to an enemy nation in a war. That is, in wartime we restrict an enemy's importation by blockade, and we encourage the enemy to export bombs, bullets, and artillery shells.

Attacking both ourselves and others at the same time doesn't seem to be a good way to conduct a war. And I didn't even know that certain members of the US Senate were planning a war against China. Although I shouldn't be surprised. In reference to the superpowers of the eighteenth century, Britain and France, Smith wrote, 'Being neighbours, they are necessarily enemies.'[17] And nowadays we're all neighbors in the global village.

Smith thought that a nation should 'regard the riches of its neighbours, as a probable cause and occasion for itself to acquire riches'.[18] But he didn't think this attitude was likely to take hold:

Each nation has been made to look with an invidious eye upon the prosperity of all the nations with which it trades, and to consider their gain as its own loss. Commerce, which ought naturally to be, among nations, as among individuals, a bond of union and friendship, has become the most fertile source of discord and animosity.[19]

So maybe we will end up in armed conflict with China – the Consumer Electronic Goods Wars, with Chinese gunboats cruising the fountains in our malls. But even if war comes we shouldn't worry that the Chinese have all our money. 'Fleets and armies are maintained, not with gold and silver,' Smith wrote, 'but with consumable goods.'[20] Oops, we should worry. The Chinese are making all our consumable goods. Our unfavorable balance of trade with China has destroyed our industrial infrastructure. We don't have the factories and skilled workers to fight a major war.

And yet, as of this writing, America is fighting a war anyway. And it's turned out to be fairly major. And America's helicopter gunships are not being assembled in Guangdong Province.

Military power depends on economic success. Economic success depends on freedom. 'No regulation of commerce,' Smith wrote, 'can increase the quantity of industry in any society ... It can only divert a part of it into a direction into which it might not otherwise have gone.'[21] Trust to capitalism that industry would have gone in that direction already, if more economic success was to be found there. Schumer and Graham should shut up. That was Smith's most important public policy recommendation for achieving economic success: 'The law ought always to trust people with the care of their own interest, as ... they must generally be able to judge better of it than the legislator can do.'[22]

A negative balance of trade, Smith declared, does not invalidate that rule:

> A nation may import to a greater value than it exports for
> half a century ... even the debts too which it contracts in
> the principal nations with whom it deals, may be gradually
> increasing; and yet its real wealth, the exchangeable value

of the annual produce of its lands and labour, may, during the same period, have been increasing in a much greater proportion.[23]

America's would-be neomercantilists might be surprised by the example Smith used to prove his point:

The state of our North American colonies, and of the trade which they carried on with Great Britain, before the commencement of the present disturbances, may serve as a proof that this is by no means an impossible supposition.[24]

In 1776, Britain was the most powerful country on earth. The reason for this, wrote Smith, was plain. 'That security which the laws in Great Britain give to every man that he shall enjoy the fruits of his own labour, is alone sufficient to make any country flourish.'[25] Restrictions of this enjoyment – including restrictions about enjoying a weekend on the couch fiddling with the remote for a plasma TV made in China – do not enhance the flourishing.

In 1776, Britain was so powerful that it could be defeated only by a people intent on establishing laws that would give them even more security for even more enjoyment of all the fruit they could eat.

The Wealth of Nations, Book 4, Continued: Adam Smith versus the Ideological Swine When They Were Still Cute, Squealing Piglets

The mercantilists were not Adam Smith's only target. Book 4 of *Wealth* also presents a polite (but not very) attack on the French physiocrats. Smith was friends with members of the physiocratic school. He admired their founder, court physician François Quesnay, enough that it was his intention to dedicate *The Wealth of Nations* to him. But Quesnay died shortly before publication. Maybe it was just as well, considering what was said about the physiocrats in *Wealth*. Smith also respected the abilities of Quesnay's two most prominent disciples, Anne-Robert-Jacques Turgot, who was Louis XVI's comptroller of finances, and Pierre-Samuel Du Pont de Nemours, who became an economic advisor to the French revolutionary government until he was denounced for being insufficiently radical.

The principles of the physiocrats were so insufficiently radical that, on first hearing, they sound like those of country club

Republicans or provincial Tories. The physiocrats believed in private property, minimal government, and bureaucratic noninterference. A precursor to the physiocrats, Vincent de Gournay – whom they regarded as a sort of John the Baptist of their thinking – coined the term *laissez-faire*. The physiocrats respected the law. When Louis XVI was the dauphin, Quesnay advised him that, upon becoming king, he should 'do nothing, but let the laws rule'. It was sad advice considering the laws the Jacobins would pass. But, then again, the physiocrats always were skeptical about popular democracy.

The physiocrats referred to themselves as *economists* and were the first students of economy to claim that honorific. Until then *economist* meant someone who was good at scrimping and saving. The physiocrats were also the first to formulate a coherent economic theory. Adam Smith agreed with all the economic deductions the physiocrats made. He agreed with everything concerning their theory, except the theory.

The physiocrats applied far too much power of ratiocination to the concepts of 'productive' and 'unproductive' labor. The distinction between the two was silly enough in Adam Smith's later and more measured analysis, but the physiocrats were obsessed with the subject. They convinced themselves that, as Smith summarized it, 'The labour of artificers and manufacturers never adds any thing to the value of the whole annual amount of the rude produce of the land,' and 'Mercantile stock is equally barren and unproductive.'[1] For increasing the wealth of a nation, farming was all that mattered. However, the physiocrats decided that mining was helpful, too. So they made mining a part of farming, as if French peasants digging turnips could just dig a little deeper and get iron ore and coal.

To the physiocrats, occupations other than farming were considered 'sterile' and yet, at the same time, 'useful'. They did not propose to restrict trade or manufacturing. The physiocrats held that, again in Smith's words, 'It can never be the interest of the proprietors and cultivators to restrain or to discourage in any respect the industry of merchants, artificers and manufacturers.'[2] So the physiocrats recognized the importance of trade and manufacturing, but didn't recognize it. This put them on the same plane of understanding as the mercantilists, who realized 'trade enriched the country ... but how, or in what manner, none of them well knew.'

Smith disproved the physiocrats' theory in several dull pages. He could have saved himself the effort with one well-chosen word, but *bullshit* didn't come into use as an expletive until the early twentieth century.

There was something about the physiocrats, however, that bothered Smith more than the fact that they were wrong. Smith believed the economy was shaped by the nature of man. The physiocrats believed the nature of man was shaped by the economy. They thought that trading and manufacturing countries could get richer solely by economics in the older sense – hoarding income to produce more capital – while agricultural countries could get richer by growing more food, making everyone fat and happy with no hoarding necessary. Smith detailed the physiocratic thinking:

Nations, therefore, which, like France or England, consist in a great measure of proprietors and cultivators, can be enriched by industry and enjoyment. Nations, on the contrary, which, like Holland and Hamburgh, are composed chiefly of merchants, artificers and manufacturers, can grow rich only through parsimony and privation. As the interest of nations so differently circumstanced, is very different, so is likewise the common character of the people. In those of the former kind, liberality, frankness, and good fellowship, naturally make a part of that common character. In the latter, narrowness, meanness, and a selfish disposition, averse to all social pleasure and enjoyment.[3]

The passage is a rare example of sarcasm from Adam Smith. He was a Scot, and what prosperity Scotland had it owed to merchants, artificers, and manufacturers. The wholly agricultural areas of Scotland were almost as grim and feudal as they had been at the time of the Highland rising. Smith lived in England for six years while he studied at Oxford. His experience could not be described as one of social pleasure and enjoyment. France was a scene of deprivation, despotism, and intrigue and was rife with the bad fellowship that would lead to the French Revolution. Holland and Hamburg were the wealthiest places in Europe, well populated with comfortable bourgeois famous for their domestic felicities.

Smith also considered the physiocrats to be too caught up in idealism for their own, or anyone's, good. According to Smith (in a second example of sarcasm) the physiocrats believed that 'the establishment of perfect justice, of perfect liberty, and of perfect equality, is the very simple secret which most effectually secures the highest degree of prosperity.'[4] But, wrote Smith, 'If a nation could not prosper without the enjoyment of perfect liberty and perfect justice, there is not in the world a nation which could ever have prospered.'[5]

Adam Smith is commonly treated as if, like the physiocrats, he had an economic theory. There are many theories in *The Wealth of Nations* but no theoretical system that Smith wanted to put in place except 'the obvious and simple system of natural liberty [that] establishes itself of its own accord'.[6]

The physiocrats not only had a theoretical system but regarded it, the way Marxists would later regard Marxism, as essential. Smith quoted another of Quesnay's disciples, the Marquis de Mirabeau, on the 'three great inventions which have principally given stability to political societies'.[7] These the marquis listed as writing, money, and Quesnay's Tableau Économique.

The danger of theoretical systems was something that Smith addressed with his own theory in part 6 of *The Theory of Moral Sentiments*. This section of the book was actually written after *The Wealth of Nations. Moral Sentiments* had been published in 1759 when Smith was teaching at Glasgow. But Smith revised it in 1789. By then he had met the physiocrats and had been exposed to their system of political economy. In part 6, titled 'Of the Character of Virtue', Smith located the evil of political systems in – per the great theme of *Moral Sentiments* – lack of imagination. Creating a theoretical political system does take imagination, but, Smith argued, there's an unimaginative side to putting it into practice:

> From a certain spirit of system … we sometimes seem to val-ue the means more than the end, and to be eager to promote the happiness of our fellow-creatures, rather from a view to perfect and improve a certain beautiful and orderly system, than from any immediate sense or feeling of what they either suffer or enjoy.[8]

Theorizers, Smith wrote, can become 'intoxicated with the imaginary beauty of this ideal system'[9] until 'that public spirit which is founded upon the love of humanity'[10] is corrupted by a spirit of system that 'inflames it even to the madness of fanaticism'.[11]

The physiocrats were moderate, inoffensive, and well meaning. But in the artificiality of their oversystematic sys-tem and in their idea that artificial systems change men, were the seeds of a hundred million murders. And their foolish doctrines about agricultural land would drive the colonial atrocities of the Victorian era and abet the kaiser's First World War, the führer's Second, Stalin's ruination of the Ukraine, and Mao's starvation of China. In the two centuries after the physiocrats, more people would die from excesses of theory than had died from excesses of theology in all the centuries before. (And, in another small matter of seed, the son of the mild physiocrat marquis was the French Revolution's fiery Mirabeau.)

Before totalitarianism had ever been tried, Adam Smith was prescient in his scorn for it:

> The man of system ... is apt to be very wise in his own conceit; and is often so enamored with the supposed beauty of his own ideal plan of government, that he cannot suffer the smallest deviation from any part of it ... He seems to imagine that he can arrange the different members of a great society with as much ease as the hand arranges the different pieces upon a chess-board.[12]

Barbed wire always seems to be needed to keep the chessmen on their squares.

Part 6 of *Moral Sentiments* is often read as referring to the constitution makers of the National Assembly in the early days of the French Revolution, rather than to the physiocrats. The Tennis Court Oath took place on June 20, 1789. Smith's revisions of *Moral Sentiments* were supposed to be sent to his publisher the same month. Assuming that Smith was late with his manuscript, as authors sometimes are, there was just time for both readings of part 6 to be true.

But if Smith was criticizing the French Revolution, he never knew how right he was. Smith died in July 1790, with the beheadings of France's king and queen and the Reign of Terror still in the future. The full ugliness of secular ideology wasn't evident to Adam Smith. Quarrels over 'place' – on earth or in heaven – were still the main worry of sensible eighteenth-century political observers.

Smith could take a detached view of theoretical political systems and, with no foreknowledge of the League of Nations or the Nazis, declare, 'Even the weakest and the worst of them are not altogether without their utility.'[13]

Smith was firm in his contradiction of the physiocratic school but gentle with the physiocrats. In *The Wealth of Nations* he called their theory 'this liberal and generous system'.[14] And declared it to be, 'perhaps, the nearest approximation to the truth that has yet been published upon the subject of political economy'.[15] (Smith's own, of course, was still awaiting publication.)

Smith's approximation to the truth was, mercifully, more approximate. *The Wealth of Nations* is less an **R** than a diagnosis. It is mostly free of those perfect abstractions for which men kill and die. It's hard to picture a furious mob mounting the barricades and shouting, as they fall upon the gendarmerie, 'OF THE CAUSES OF IMPROVEMENT IN THE PRODUCTIVE POWERS OF LABOUR, AND OF THE ORDER ACCORDING TO WHICH ITS PRODUCE IS NATURALLY DISTRIBUTED AMONG THE DIFFERENT RANKS OF THE PEOPLE!!!'

Smith should have been tougher on the physiocrats. He should have heeded his friend David Hume. Hume wanted to 'thunder them, and crush them, and pound them, and reduce them to dust and ashes'.[16]

CHAPTER 10

Adam Smith, America's Founding Dutch Uncle

Adam Smith didn't live to see the French Revolution. But he witnessed a revolution of a very different kind: 'When in the Course of human events, it becomes necessary for one people to dissolve the political bands which have connected them with another ...' This wasn't really a revolution at all. It was a provincial flare-up between freeborn Englishmen. But it would change human life more, and more hopefully, than all the radical and fanatic revolutions that were to come.

Smith was interested in the American colonies and the 'present disturbances' there. The index to *The Wealth of Nations* contains more than a hundred entries under 'America'. Smith devotes a long chapter in book 4 of *Wealth* to the political philosophy of colonies in general and to the causes of the rebellion in a particular thirteen of them. In book 5, where the ways and means of government were considered, Smith returns to the subject. The last pages of *The Wealth of Nations* are given over to a consideration of Britain's colonial empire.

Something should be said about Smith's use of the word *empire*. Sadly for the history of meaning in language, we owe our present-day definition of *imperialism* to Lenin. Frustrated by capitalism's continued failure to impoverish its proletariat and then collapse, Lenin decided that capitalism had been 'transformed into imperialism'[1] in order to 'plunder the whole world'[2] instead of just the local working class.

Adam Smith's name for this was mercantilism. Smith knew the classics, as did his readers. In Latin, *imperator* simply means the holder of a chief military command. In the Roman republic it was an honorary title, bestowed on a victorious general by acclamation of his troops. The Roman Empire, as originally conceived, was supposed to have an *imperator,* not a *rex.* Julius Caesar accepted the political appointment of emperor but refused the hereditary office of king. There were no 'evil empires' extant in Smith's time, only a couple of decaying and ineffective ones, the Chinese and the Holy Roman. Smith was free to employ the term *empire* in a neutral or even an optimistically figurative sense, as his friend David Hume did in his essay 'The Sceptic': 'The empire of philosophy extends over a few.'[3]

Albeit Smith was not philosophically optimistic about the British Empire, especially not about the colonial American part of it. The ruling classes, he warned, must either understand the proper nature of an empire in North America or suffer the consequences 'in the case of a total separation from Great Britain, which … seems very likely'.[4]

Smith was considered enough of an expert on America that in 1778 the British government sought his advice. General John Burgoyne had surrendered at Saratoga the previous fall, and the American war was going poorly or, as an American would say, well. Smith wrote a detailed memorandum to a member of Lord Frederick North's cabinet, Alexander Wedderburn, who had been a friend of Smith's for thirty years.

Historians did not discover this document until the 1930s. By the time it came to light Smith's comments seemed more pertinent to the too feeble Britain of the twentieth century than the too masterful Britain of the eighteenth:

> A government which, in times of the most profound peace, of the highest public prosperity, when the people had scarce even the pretext of a single grievance to complain of, has not always been able to make itself respected by them; would have every thing to fear from their rage and indignation at the public disgrace and calamity ... of thus dismembering the empire.[5]

'Rage and indignation' at the governing classes is probably as good an explanation as any for how Britain, the original laboratory of the obvious and simple system of natural liberty, got itself into the socialist pickle from which it has yet to be fully extracted. But another, larger lab experiment was about to be conducted on the other side of the ocean.

Smith predicted to Wedderburn that the Americans would reject the type of conciliation with the parent country that Edmund Burke had proposed in 1775. And Smith predicted that if Britain continued the American war it would lose, even if it won: 'A military government would naturally be established there; and the ... Americans ... will, for more than a century to come, be at all times ready to take arms in order to overturn it.'[6] Smith predicted the war's outcome: 'The submission or conquest of a part, but of a part only, of America, seems ... by far the most probable.'[7] That is, Britain got to keep Canada. And Smith predicted the outcome's outcome: 'yet the similarity of language and manners would in most cases dispose the Americans to prefer our alliance to that of any other nation.'[8]

None of these predictions, except the last, pleased Smith. But he had a cool and detached – one might say an Impartial Spectator's – view of the conflict.

In *The Wealth of Nations*, Smith expressed moral and utilitarian objections to what our modern, more ostentatiously moral (if less useful) thinkers call colonialism:

> Folly and injustice seem to have been the principles which presided over and directed the first project of establishing those colonies; the folly of hunting after gold and silver mines, and the injustice of coveting the possession of a country whose harmless natives, far from having ever injured the people of Europe, had received the first adventurers with every mark of kindness and hospitality.[9]

Smith was unmodern in applying the pejorative 'harmless' to Native Americans. He was more so in his opinions that 'the present grandeur of the colonies of America'[10] was an improvement on pre-Columbian conditions despite 'the savage injustice of the Europeans ... ruinous and destructive to several of these unfortunate countries'.[11] Smith was also unmodern in crediting colonial accomplishments to Western civilization instead of, say, Pocahontas: 'the colonies owe to ... Europe the education and great views of their active and enterprising founders.'[12] But Smith gave Western civilization negative as well as positive credit: 'It was, not the wisdom and policy, but the disorder and injustice of the European governments, which peopled and cultivated America.'[13] The lack of opportunities at home, not the abundance of opportunities overseas, caused the colonies to grow.

Smith was critical of the British government with its 'mean and malignant expedients of the mercantile system'[14] whose trade restrictions were 'impertinent badges of slavery'[15] imposed on the Americans 'without any sufficient reason, by the groundless jealousy of the merchants and manufacturers of the mother country'.[16]

Smith was so infuriated by the trade restrictions on the American colonies that, uncharacteristically, he indulged himself in a protracted jeremiad – his 'nation of shopkeepers' tirade.

The slur that Britain was nothing more than that is often attributed to the diminutive Corsican who was soon to give the British more trouble even than the Americans. But it was a common phrase, used to describe any commercial nation. Louis XIV is supposed to have said it about the Dutch. Note that Smith didn't think the leaders of his country rose anywhere near to the level of being shopkeepers:

To found a great empire for the sole purpose of raising up a people of customers, may at first sight appear a project fit only for a nation of shopkeepers. It is, however, a project altogether unfit for a nation of shopkeepers; but extremely fit for a nation whose government is influenced by shopkeepers. Such statesmen, and such statesmen only, are capable of fancying that they will find some advantage in employing the blood and treasure of their fellow citizens, to found and maintain such an empire. Say to a shopkeeper, Buy me a good estate, and I shall always buy my clothes at your shop, even though I should pay somewhat dearer than what I can have them for at other shops; and you will not find him very forward to embrace your proposal. But should any other person buy you such an estate, the shopkeeper would be much obliged to your benefactor if he would enjoin you to buy all your clothes at his shop. [And so on for two pages until the diatribe ends in exasperation:] Under the present system of management, therefore, Great Britain derives nothing but loss from the dominion which she assumes over her colonies.[17]

The inspiration for this philippic was, however, the only thing about the American Revolution that Smith found inspirational. We Americans are stirred by the political thinking of our national patriarchs. Adam Smith was not.

Smith was an idealist but he did not have the Romantic's faith in pure ideas, the faith which was beginning to take hold in France and, indeed, in America. Smith did not think so highly of ideas that when he saw a good thing he automatically thought a good idea had caused it. God moves in a mysterious way, let alone Massachusetts.

Smith was critical of the colonists. He considered them to be not so much sterling patriots as skinflints with their sterling: 'The English colonists have never yet contributed any thing towards the defence of the mother country, or towards the support of its civil government. They themselves, on the contrary, have hitherto been defended almost entirely at the expence of the mother country.'[18]

In Smith's memorandum to Wedderburn the brilliance of Thomas Jefferson, James Madison, Alexander Hamilton, Thomas Paine, et al., was dismissed in one sentence: 'In their present elevation of spirits, the ulcerated minds of the Americans are not likely to consent to any union even upon terms the most advantageous to themselves.'[19]

Smith detected the ordinary self-seeking – 'by no means the weak side of human nature' – behind America's revolutionary idealism. In *The Wealth of Nations* he debunked the Founding Fathers:

The persons who now govern the resolutions of what they call their continental congress, feel in themselves at this moment a degree of importance which, perhaps the greatest subjects in Europe scarce feel. From shopkeepers, tradesmen, and attorneys, they are become statesmen and legislators, and are employed in contriving a new form of government.[20]

Smith did not regard that new form of government as an opportunity for mankind to achieve splendid new social ideals. Smith saw America as a practical problem. We Americans, the most practical of people, might pay attention to Smith's perspective on the American Revolution. We might doff some of our idealistic trappings, look in the political mirror, and see ourselves for what we are, a practical solution.

Even in the heady days leading up to the Declaration of Independence there was a prosaic and businesslike aspect to the American Revolution. The French Revolution did not get its start in a tiff over customs duties. The sans-culottes were not middle-class entrepreneurs like Paul Revere and Sam Adams, and running around without pants they weren't likely to become so. The Jacobins didn't put on feather bonnets to stage a commercial protest. If there ever had been a Paris Tea Party, the revolutionaries wouldn't have been dumping oolong, they would have been scalping everyone in sight and then each other. No beer is named after Dr Guillotin.

To the practical problem of America, Adam Smith had a practical solution – get out of there. 'Great Britain should voluntarily give up all authority over her colonies, and leave them to elect their own magistrates, to enact their own laws, and to make peace and war as they might think proper ... It might dispose them ... to favour us in war as well as in trade, and, instead of turbulent and factious subjects, to become our most faithful, affectionate, and generous allies.'[21] (Which, though Smith's advice was not followed, America has turned out to be, except in 1812, and during the Civil War, and when we were feeling neutral about Germany in the nineteen-teens and the nineteen-thirties, and in the Suez crisis, and anytime a question of Ireland has been involved.)

Smith didn't think his practical solution was practical. He called it 'a measure as never was, and never will be adopted, by any nation in the world'.[22] Smith's perceptions about why 'Peace Now' always falls on deaf ears still apply. The current political reality in Tibet, Chechnya, the West Bank, and maybe, alas, Baghdad was accurately described by Adam Smith:

> No nation ever voluntarily gave up the dominion of any
> province, how troublesome soever it might be to govern
> it ... Such sacrifices, though they might frequently be
> agreeable to the interest, are always mortifying to the pride
> of every nation, and what is perhaps of still greater conse-
> quence, they are always contrary to the private interest of
> the governing part of it, who would thereby be deprived
> of the disposal of many places of trust and profit, of many
> opportunities of acquiring wealth and distinction, which the
> possession of the most turbulent, and, to the great body of
> the people, the most unprofitable province seldom fails to
> afford.[23]

Smith had another even less practical solution to the American problem, a merger with Great Britain. Benjamin Franklin had proposed such an idea in the 1750s, but tempers had been cooler then. Smith seemed to feel that he was now almost the only person in favor of it. He told Wedderburn that political agglomeration 'seems scarce to have a single advocate ... if you except here and there a solitary philosopher like myself'.[24]

Nonetheless in *The Wealth of Nations,* Smith wrote that he thought making America part of Great Britain 'can at worst be regarded but as a new Utopia, less amusing certainly, but not more useless and chimerical than the old one'.[25] He was citing the same work of visionary fiction that he'd earlier mocked. There's something about America, prosaic as the place and its populace may be, that makes people dream. Smith told Wedderburn, 'The plan ... would certainly tend most to the prosperity, to the splendour, and to the duration of the empire.'[26] Smith argued the advantages of Anglo-American union in book 4 of *Wealth* and again in book 5, making a total of a dozen references to the subject. He thought that his concept could be extended 'to all the different provinces of the empire inhabited by people of either British or European extraction'.[27] (Lest this be thought racist, he favored including the Irish.) He even foresaw, without wincing, the Bush/Blair relationship:

> In the course of little more than a century, perhaps, the produce of American might exceed that of British taxation. The seat of the empire would then naturally remove itself to that part of the empire which contributed most to the general defence and support of the whole.[28]

If Smith's dream had been effected sooner, in 1776 instead of during the Iraq War, we'd be living in a different world. There might have been no American Civil War, world wars, Cold War, or poke-noses from the EU Commission on Everything. On the other hand, there might have been ten thousand Belfasts where 'a military government would naturally be established' and where a billion people were 'at all times ready to take arms in order to overturn it'.

As it is, we're living in a different world anyway. And it's interesting that Smith didn't have the dream about America that actually came true. The United States would prove Adam Smith's own thesis: wealth depends on division of labor; division of labor depends on trade; trade depends on natural liberty; therefore Freedom = Wealth.

If anything the United States has provided an embarrassment of proof. What will archaeologists of the distant future make of the American empire's ruins? They'll dig up SUVs obviously too big ever to have moved. They must have been for ceremonial purposes. The ubiquitous remains of swimming pools, the countless types and kinds of sneakers, and the ruins of more fast-food outlets than any estimate of twenty-first-century population can account for will convince thirty-first-century scholars that we were semiaquatic, six-legged creatures who worshipped fat in cars.

But Adam Smith was too practical a man to dream up anything that silly. And since we Americans are ourselves so practical we should heed not only what Smith had to say about our revolution but what he had to say about the thing that our revolution eventually would get us, an empire like Britain's.

The lambasting that Smith gave to the British imperialists could be given to anyone who intends to profit from an empire. It doesn't matter if the expected gain is crass – commercial prosperity – or noble – democracy. A successful empire is not an array of cowed dependencies, importunate client states, and outposts held by bribery or force. 'They may perhaps,' Smith wrote, 'be considered as appendages, as a sort of splendid and showy equipage of the empire.'[29]

Adam Smith thought that the mistakes of British imperial policy were so grave and so dangerous to individuals that he used an ardent condemnation of that policy as his final passage in *The Wealth of Nations:*

> The rulers of Great Britain have, for more than a century past, amused the people with the imagination that they possessed a great empire on the west side of the Atlantic. This empire, however, has hitherto existed in imagination only. It has hitherto been, not an empire, but the project of an empire; not a gold mine, but the project of a gold mine ... It is surely now time that our rulers should either realize this golden dream, in which they have been indulging themselves, perhaps, as well as the people; or, that they should awake from it themselves, and endeavour to awaken the people. If the project cannot be completed, it ought to be given up ... Great Britain should free herself

from the expence of defending those provinces in time of war, and of supporting any part of their civil or military establishments in time of peace, and endeavour to accommodate her future views and designs to the real mediocrity of her circumstances.[30]

The Wealth of Nations, Book 5 'Of the Revenue of the Sovereign or Commonwealth' Adam Smith, Policy Wonk

Adam Smith was human, and never more so than in book 5 of *The Wealth of Nations*. No one can resist giving advice. As a 'solitary philosopher', Adam Smith's advice was good. He applied his lofty intellect to such great political issues as the war in America. But in book 5 he also applied his intellect to mundane political issues. He yielded to the temptation to slide down Olympus.

Smith should have known better than to enmesh himself in the bureaucratic details of public policy. In *The Theory of Moral Sentiments* he warned against thinkers 'who reduced their doctrines into a ... technical system of artificial definitions, divisions, and subdivisions'.[1] Smith called this 'one of the most effectual expedients, perhaps, for extinguishing whatever degree of good sense there may be in any moral or metaphysical doctrine'.[2]

Smith risked becoming as 'wise in his own conceit' as James Carville, Karl Rove, or Anthony Giddens. Already in book 4, on the subject of Spanish versus British colonies, Smith had embraced the central fallacy of the political advisor, the same fallacy he'd detected in the physiocrats: 'what forms the character of every nation, the nature of their government'.[3] By the middle of book 5 Smith was holding forth like a world-weary Washington insider after a day full of the momentarily momentous policy crises beloved of world-weary Washington insiders:

> For though management and persuasion are always the easi-est and the safest instruments of government, as force and violence are the worst and the most dangerous, yet such, it seems, is the natural insolence of man, that he almost always disdains to use the good instrument, except when he cannot or dare not use the bad one.[4]

The mundane political issues of Smith's time were – it is sad to discover – exactly the same as ours: law and order, politi-cal pork, failures of the educational system, religion in politics, Byzantine tax code, burgeoning national debt, and runaway defense spending. Two and a quarter centuries of intractabil-ity in these policy matters would seem to indicate a certain ... intractability.

If we reconciled ourselves to this intractability, the modern overpopulation of political advisors, commentators, and ex-perts could be culled. Space could be opened up in the *New*

York Times for more lingerie ads. And Sunday morning TV partisan blather could be replaced with reruns of *Curb Your Enthusiasm*. If we wanted to have an opinion about some pressing issue, we could read book 5 of *Wealth* and spout the mixed-up pronouncements of Adam Smith.

'Of the Expence of Justice'

Despite the title of this section, Smith didn't have much to say about the expense of justice other than that it's expensive. 'Justice, however, never was in reality administered gratis in any country,'[5] wrote Smith, putting a more dignified gloss on the comment of actor and murder suspect Robert Blake who said he was 'innocent until proven broke'.

Smith lamented that the origin of judicial systems had more to do with sovereign revenue than sovereign fairness: 'The persons who applied to [the king] for justice were always willing to pay for it ... This scheme of making the administration of justice subservient to the purposes of revenue, could scarce fail to be productive of several very gross abuses.'[6] I'm thinking of speeding tickets in a certain New Hampshire small town which I won't name because I live there.

I'll have to drive more slowly because Smith, like the political analysts of today, was at his best with the big picture. Smith was articulate on the enormous question, what is the abstract nature of justice? He was not so articulate on the small question, how do I get some?

Adam Smith was so articulate on the abstract nature of justice that he could have gone into a television studio by himself and been the host and all the guests on a Fox News show.

'Civil government ... is in reality instituted for the defence of the rich against the poor,'[7] Smith wrote, sounding like the obligatory left-wing nut guest.

Then he sounded like the right-wing nut host: 'in the poor the hatred of labour and the love of present ease and enjoyment, are the passions which prompt to invade property.'[8]

Then the left-wing nut again: 'Wherever there is great property, there is great inequality.'[9]

And then the guest who is even more of a right-wing nut than the host and who has had too much coffee: 'It is only under the shelter of the civil magistrate that the owner of that valuable property ... can sleep a single night in security. He is at all times surrounded by unknown enemies, whom, though he never provoked, he can never appease.'[10]

It all comes down to campaign strategies in the end. These civil magistrates, these politicos – laying down the law and meting out justice – who will they be? In choosing political leaders, Smith ruled out 'qualifications of the mind', which he considered to be 'always disputable, and generally disputed'.[11] (As if qualifications of the mind were ever a factor in politics.) And successful businessmen are not the best candidates, because, Smith opined, 'authority of fortune ... has been the constant complaint of every period of society.'[12] (Plus so many rich people have been going to jail lately, not that that distinguishes them from politicians.) Smith thought chronological age had something to recommend it, being 'a plain and palpable quality which admits of no dispute'.[13] In politics you can still be a fresh face and full of potential at fifty-three – Smith's age when *Wealth of Nations* was published. But what Smith favored most in political leaders was 'superiority of birth ... antiquity either of wealth, or of that greatness which is commonly either founded upon wealth, or accompanied with it'.[14] Smith believed that such a person's 'birth and fortune ... naturally procure him some sort of ... authority'.[15]

What an incredibly archaic opinion. Maybe Smith isn't fit for appearances on modern media after all. Unless you consider the pair of blue-blooded bums on the plush who ran for president of the United States in 2004.

Doubtless Smith would have positioned himself as being above vulgar politics. Perhaps he would have supported both Bush and Kerry. But he couldn't have expected much abstract justice from what either of them wanted to do to the Supreme Court: 'When the judicial is united to the executive power,' Smith wrote, 'it is scarce possible that justice should not frequently be sacrificed to, what is vulgarly called, politics.'[16]

Smith did have one concrete suggestion to improve the justice system: competing law courts, where 'each court endeavoured, by superior dispatch and impartiality, to draw to itself as many causes as it could.'[17] This is a great idea – for a TV show. It's done wonders for Judge Judy, if not for the United States Court of Appeals.

'Of the Public Works and Institutions for facilitating the Commerce of Society'

Nothing about pork barrel politics has changed since the eighteenth century. This is clear from a statement that Adam Smith felt compelled to make: 'A great bridge cannot be thrown over a river at a place where nobody passes, or merely to embellish the view from the windows of a neighbouring palace.'[18] He was using the verb *cannot* in the strictly political sense, its meaning unrelated to *won't*. The next words in Smith's sentence are 'things which sometimes happen'.

Smith made an incontrovertible pronouncement about the funding of public works: 'The greater part of such ... may easily be so managed, as to afford a particular revenue sufficient for defraying their own expence.'[19] And he made an incontrovertible pronouncement that there was no hope in hell of getting that funding to go where it was supposed to: 'In the progress of despotism the authority of the executive power gradually absorbs that of every other power in the state, and assumes to itself the management of every branch of revenue.'[20]

Smith understood the potential of privatization: 'Public services are never better performed than when their reward comes only in consequence of their being performed, and is proportioned to the diligence employed in performing them.'[21] But his experience of the corporations that were contracted to perform British government services – such as the East India Company, the Halliburton of its day – left him too skeptical to suggest privatization: 'These companies ... have in the long-run proved, universally, either burdensome or useless.'[22]

All that Smith could do about pork barrel projects was voice the kind of feckless common sense that never influences politics: 'they can be made only where that commerce requires them, and ... their grandeur and magnificence, must be suited to what that commerce can afford to pay.'[23] He would have been helpless to prevent the recent US highway transportation bill with its $200 million bridge in Ketchikan, Alaska (population 7,410). But at least Smith wouldn't have proposed a Millennium Dome in London or vast housing estates for malcontents in the suburbs of Paris or rebuilding slums below sea level so college kids have a place to get drunk during Mardi Gras.

'Of the Expence of the Institutions for
the Education of Youth'

Any discussion of educational policy quickly turns into a blow-top session. Everyone's been stuffed with sixteen or twenty years of school, is full to the brim, and ready to spew. Smith was no exception, calling universities 'the sanctuaries in which exploded systems and obsolete prejudices found shelter and protection, after they had been hunted out of every other corner of the world'.[24]

Smith propounded his educational theories. He was in favor of more science: 'The proper subject of experiment and observation, a subject in which a careful attention is capable of making so many useful discoveries.'[25] He was against subjects 'in which, after a few very simple and almost obvious truths, the most careful attention can discover nothing but obscurity and uncertainty'.[26] He was referring to metaphysics, but we can substitute poststructuralist minority feminist gay literary criticism and take his point. He cited, approvingly, the ancient Greek curriculum of 'physics, or natural philosophy; ethics, or moral philosophy; and logic', maintaining that 'this general division seems perfectly agreeable to the nature of things.'[27] Although I'm not sure where Auto Shop, Phys Ed, and lunch would fit in. And he denounced ontology, calling it 'this cobweb science',[28] which was a relief to me because I got a D on that quiz in Introduction to Philosophy.

But reasonable opinions go only so far on educational issues. Smith was soon in controversial territory. He was opposed to making education wholly free, lest students get what they paid for. And he protested against government control of schools: 'An extraneous jurisdiction of this kind ... is liable to be exercised both ignorantly and capriciously.'[29] Smith, a teacher himself, knew what political pressure does to teachers:

> The person subject to such jurisdiction is necessarily degraded by it, and, instead of being one of the most respectable, is rendered one of the meanest and most contemptible persons in the society. It is by powerful protection only that he can effectually guard himself

against the bad usage to which he is at all times exposed; and this protection he is most likely to gain, not by ability or diligence in his profession, but by obsequiousness to the will of his superiors.[30]

Otherwise known as joining a teachers' union and voting for liberal Democrats.

Smith assailed compulsory education as well. 'There are no public institutions for the education of women,' he wrote, 'and there is accordingly nothing useless, absurd, or fantastical in the common course of their education.'[31] You didn't catch eighteenth-century housewives bursting into angry tears during book group discussions of *Are Men Necessary?* They couldn't read.

Smith touted private schools. He claimed that 'those parts of education ... for the teaching of which there are no public institutions, are generally the best taught.'[32] As examples he gave 'a fencing or a dancing school'.[33] But I've got three children and they spend enough time waltzing around taking pokes at each other.

In heated dispute with Smith on all these points was Smith. He advocated an educational requirement 'to be undergone by every person before he was permitted to exercise any liberal profession'.[34] He called for taxpayer funding of schools: 'some attention of government is necessary in order to prevent the almost entire corruption and degeneracy of the great body of the people.'[35] And he wanted national curriculum standards: 'Science is the great antidote to the poison of enthusiasm and superstition.'[36]

Neither of Smith's educational agendas has worked. That is, all the arguments he made against public education are true. And all the arguments he made in favor of public education haven't prevented the almost entire corruption and degeneracy of the great body of the people, at least when they're watching *American Idol*. Nor has science been a great antidote for enthusiasm, such as Iran's for building an atomic bomb, or for superstition. The lotto jackpot number last week was my locker combination in high school.

We get as confused reading what Adam Smith wrote about education as he got writing it. Doubtless part of the confusion was due to the fact of Smith's being a teacher and knowing the truth about school. 'No better method, it seems, could be fallen upon of spending, with any advantage, the long interval between infancy and that period of life at which men begin to apply in good earnest to the real business of the world,'[37] he wrote. The secret to education is that we don't know what else to do with the kids.

'Of the Expence of the Institutions for the Instruction of People of all Ages'

Adam Smith may have been first to realize that politics needs a euphemism for 'church'. There's something very contemporary about 'Institutions for the Instruction of People of all

Ages', giving equal weight to pottery classes, yoga, mass, and shul. Smith was unreservedly in favor of separation of all these things and state.

> Articles of faith, as well as all other spiritual matters … are
> not within the proper department of a temporal sovereign,
> who, though he may be very well qualified for protecting, is
> seldom supposed to be so for instructing the people.[38]

Except, in the case of the future King Charles, in matters of organic farming.

And yet, as with education, Smith felt the need to explore additional policy options. On the one hand, separation of church and state was definitely good. On the other hand, maybe the government *should* fund religion. (It was this kind of thing that would cause Harry Truman to plead for a one-armed economist.) Smith quoted David Hume about how the 'interested diligence of the clergy is what every wise legislator will study to prevent'.[39] If a preacher has to support himself, he'll need, said Hume, 'to excite the languid devotion of his audience. No regard will be paid to truth, morals, or decency in the doctrines inculcated. Every tenet will be adopted that best suits the disorderly affections of the human frame.'[40] Therefore, according to Hume, what the government should do with 'spiritual guides' – in order to avoid an al-Qaeda – 'is to bribe their indolence, by assigning stated salaries to their profession'.[41, 42]

But that would mean underwriting all sorts of oddballs such as hymn-blabbing Methodists, congregation-dunking Baptists, and who knows what. So, on yet a third hand, maybe the Church of England ought to be preserved. 'This system of church government,' Smith wrote, 'was from the beginning favourable to peace and good order.'[43]

Probably there wasn't anything to be done about the separation of church and state anyway. Smith claimed that a government with no official religion was something 'such as positive law has perhaps never yet established, and probably never will establish in any country'.[44] Then, in the next paragraph, he explained just how positive law could establish it, 'provided those sects were sufficiently numerous, and each of them consequently too small to disturb the public tranquillity … and if the government was perfectly decided both to let them all alone, and to oblige them all to let alone one another'.[45] That was how we got separation of church and state in America, a country founded by religious lunatics.

Smith was also unreservedly for freedom of belief, though not in a way calculated to please believers:

The teachers of each little sect, finding themselves almost alone, would be obliged to respect those of almost every other sect, and the concessions which they would mutually find it both convenient and agreeable to make to one another, might in time probably reduce the doctrine of the greater part of them to that pure and rational religion, free from every mixture of absurdity, imposture, or fanaticism, such as wise men have in all ages of the world wished to see established.[46]

This sounds like the joke about what you get when you cross a Jehovah's Witness with a Unitarian – somebody who goes door-to-door for no reason.

And Smith had a kind of praise for fundamentalist Christians that would infuriate all of them, from Ralph Reed to Al Sharpton:

A man of low condition … is far from being a distinguished member of any great society … His conduct never excites so much the attention of any respectable society, as by his becoming the member of a small religious sect. He from that moment acquires a degree of consideration which he never had before.[47]

And don't get Smith started on Roman Catholicism: 'The most formidable combination that ever was formed against the authority and security of civil government, as well as against the liberty, reason, and happiness of mankind.'[48]

It wouldn't be a good idea to send Adam Smith out on the campaign trail, drumming up the religious vote.

'Of Taxes'

Adam Smith did a lot of thinking about taxes, eighty-odd pages worth. He began with four sensible maxims of taxation: taxes ought to be inexpensive to collect, be levied when taxpayers are best able to pay them, be proportionate to the revenue that taxpayers 'enjoy under the protection of the state',[49] and be 'certain, and not arbitrary'.[50]

The last maxim is the most sensible and therefore the least observed. The boggling complexity of tax law and the cease-less fiddling with taxes, even by legislators who would lower them, violate Smith's principle that 'a very considerable degree of inequality ... is not near so great an evil as a very small de-gree of uncertainty.'[51] It's a principle that applies to practically everything, as anyone who is in love or waiting for a check in the mail knows.

Smith was opposed to inheritance taxes, which are almost as arbitrary, if not as uncertain, as death. And they can hardly be said to be levied at a time when the taxpayer is best able to pay them, because he's dead.

Smith did not see a consumption tax as a panacea: 'All taxes upon consumable commodities ... tend to reduce the quantity of productive labour.'[52] He wouldn't have favored introducing a VAT in the United States. Just the fact that it is in use elsewhere is an argument against it. 'There is no art which one government sooner learns of another, than that of draining money from the pockets of the people,' wrote Smith.[53]

Smith was against corporate taxes because 'The proprietor of stock is properly a citizen of the world,'[54] and 'a tax which tended to drive away stock from any particular country, would so far tend to dry up every source of revenue, both to the sovereign and to the society.'[55] Also, Liechtenstein might end up as a world power. And it could hardly help but have territorial ambitions.

Smith made a sensible argument in favor of property taxes – but only on Republicans with inflated house values in nice neighborhoods: 'Nothing can be more reasonable than that a fund which owes its existence to the good government of the state, should be taxed peculiarly.'[56] And, since government was instituted for the defense of the rich against the poor, he called for progressive taxation: 'It is not very unreasonable that the rich should contribute to the public expence, not only in proportion to their revenue, but something more than in that proportion.'[57] But only if the government makes the poor knock it off with the graffiti and turn down the rap music.

Smith objected to certain taxes on libertarian grounds:

> It would have been impossible to proportion with tolerable exactness the tax upon a shop to the extent of the trade carried on in it, without such an inquisition as would have been altogether insupportable in a free country.[58]

We're very proud of our modern liberty, but that sentence indicates we may have dropped a few freedoms while we were stooping to pick up all the new ones.

And Smith had one really brilliant tax idea, a surcharge on 'the persons who have the administration of government'.[59] He felt that they were 'generally disposed to reward both themselves and their immediate dependents rather more than enough'.[60] St Andrews was founded in 1754, so golf junkets with lobbyists were already available. 'The emoluments of officers, therefore, can in most cases very well bear to be taxed,' wrote Smith.[61] He predicted this would be 'always a very popular tax'.[62]

Nonetheless, thinking about taxes leads to bad thinking. Think what you would do to the IRS auditor if not for the laws of God and man. And those who would recommend taxes are led as far astray as those who would avoid paying them. Smith's preferred method of raising revenue was a luxury tax. This would be imposed not only on the frivolities of the rich but on 'the luxurious [but] not the necessary expence of the inferior ranks of people'.[63]

Let us consider, on evidence that Smith himself provided, what the eighteenth century considered a poor person's 'necessary expence' to be:

> It may indeed be doubted whether butchers meat is any
> where a necessary of life. Grain and other vegetables,
> with the help of milk, cheese, and butter, or oil, where
> butter is not to be had, it is known from experience, can,
> without any butchers meat, afford the most plentiful,
> the most wholesome, the most nourishing, and the most
> invigorating diet.[64]

And let us further consider what, in Smith's words, that plentiful, wholesome, nourishing, invigorating diet actually consisted of:

> The circumstances of the poor through a great part of Eng-
> land cannot surely be so much distressed by any rise in the
> price of poultry, fish, wild-fowl, or venison, as they must be
> relieved by the fall in that of potatoes.[65]

And potatoes don't hurt poor people a bit:

> The chairmen, porters, and coal-heavers in London, and
> those unfortunate women who live by prostitution, the
> strongest men and the most beautiful women perhaps in the
> British dominions, are said to be, the greater part of them,
> from the lowest rank of people in Ireland, who are generally
> fed with this root.[66]

In the eighteenth century the poor had not yet been elevated
to their present status as a valuable source of fads, fashions, and
illegal drugs. The inferior ranks were openly considered inferior, rather than secretly and guiltily considered inferior.
Even as decent a man as Adam Smith accepted this inferiority
without giving it a decent thought. Smith, in his role as policy advisor, wrote the following without any apparent sense that he was
contradicting the most important parts of *The Wealth of Nations*:

> Upon the sober and industrious poor, taxes upon [luxuries] act
> as sumptuary laws, and dispose them either to moderate, or to
> refrain altogether from the use of superfluities which they can
> no longer easily afford. Their ability to bring up families, in

consequence of this forced frugality, instead of being dimin-
ished, is frequently, perhaps, increased by the tax'.[67]

Perhaps. But the subject of taxes can push a person beyond
being merely wrong. Smith was starting to sound slightly de-
mented when he proclaimed, 'Every tax, however, is to the person who pays it a badge, not of slavery, but of liberty. It denotes
that he is subject to government, indeed, but that, as he has some
property, he cannot himself be the property of a master.'[68] And
Smith must have been completely out of his head when he
wrote about income received by a landowner for renting land:
'Though a part of this revenue should be taken from him in
order to defray the expences of the state, no discouragement
will thereby be given to any sort of industry.'[69]

Taxes drive people crazy. Smith as much as admitted it
when he declared, rather crazily, 'After all the proper subjects
of taxation have been exhausted … they must be imposed upon
improper ones.'[70]

'Advice, n. The smallest current coin.'
  – Ambrose Bierce, *The Devil's Dictionary*

Not all of Adam Smith's policy recommendations were
worthless or self-canceling or cracked. He dismissed government ownership of businesses in one sentence: 'The state cannot
be very great of which the sovereign has leisure to carry on the
trade a wine merchant or apothecary.'[71]

He cleared the fog about national debt, which isn't a Keynesian stimulus to the economy or a Milton Friedmanish drag upon same, but a moral outrage. It allows government to indulge in sneaking:

> Every new tax is immediately felt more or less by the people. It occasions always some murmur, and meets with some opposition ... Debt is not immediately felt by the people, and occasions neither murmur nor complaint.[72]

And larceny:

> When national debts have once been accumulated to a certain degree, there is scarce, I believe, a single instance of their having been fairly and completely paid.[73]

And counterfeiting. Because the devaluation of currency that results from such defaults should properly be called ...

> ... an injustice of treacherous fraud.[74]

This inevitably leads to inflation, which ...

> ... occasions a general and most pernicious subversion of the fortunes of private people; enriching in most cases the idle and profuse debtor at the expence of the industrious and frugal creditor.[75]

So every time you cash your social security check you're buying a golf course for Donald Trump.

In 'Of the Expence of Defence' Smith advised us to be glad that defense is expensive: 'In modern war the great expence of fire-arms gives an evident advantage to the nation which can best afford that expence.'[76] This is why the Berlin Wall came down. The Star Wars missile defense didn't work, but only the United States could afford to build one to find that out. The USSR was not in an economic position to threaten America with Mutual Assured Bankruptcy.

Adam Smith would have been a first-rate National Security Advisor in the Reagan administration. But even the best advice can't always be given twice. 'The invention of fire-arms,' wrote Smith, 'an invention which at first sight appears to be so pernicious, is certainly favourable both to the permanency and to the extension of civilization.'[77] The Tigris–Euphrates river valley is the cradle of civilization. The Iraqis can afford guns.

A policy advisor, even more than the politicians he advises, should know his place. And that place should be nowhere near the economy. At the end of book 4 of *Wealth,* Smith observes, 'The sovereign is completely discharged from a duty ... for the proper performance of which no human wisdom or knowledge could ever be sufficient; the duty of superintending the industry of private people.'[78] And Smith goes on to say all that ever needs to be said about the duties that government does have:

First, the duty of protecting the society from the violence and invasion of other independent societies; secondly, the duty of protecting, as far as possible, every member of the society from the injustice or oppression of every other member of it ...; thirdly, the duty of erecting and maintaining certain public works and certain public institutions, which it can never be for the interest of any individual, or small number of individuals, to erect and maintain.[79]

And yet, on that third point, if the works and institutions aren't for the interest of any individual, why are we individuals paying to erect and maintain them? This brings us – and Adam Smith – back to politics.

CHAPTER 12

Adam Smith's Lost Book

Adam Smith didn't write his book on politics. There were a number of reasons that the third part of Smith's betterment trilogy, his work on 'jurisprudence', was never finished. He was busy making revisions to *The Theory of Moral Sentiments*. He became a government official in Scotland. He died.

But I wonder if there wasn't another reason. Smith was a moral philosopher. It may be that at some point he realized politics isn't a good place for philosophy and is no place for morals. Could it have been while he was writing book 5 of *The Wealth of Nations*? Smith's old footnote on himself in *Moral Sentiments* about being concerned with 'a matter of fact' rather than 'a matter of right' could never be applied to a consideration of politics. Politics is all about right, which is to say wrong.

Political systems are founded upon paradoxes too deep for philosophy. Adam Smith was aware of this when he was writing *Moral Sentiments* in the 1750s. He alluded to it in the first chapter: 'A prison is certainly more useful to the public than a palace; and a person who founds the one is generally directed by a much juster spirit of patriotism, than he who builds the other.'[1] Yet no father says to a newborn baby, 'Someday you may be warden of Leavenworth.'

The best intentions of political systems are refuted by dilemma. Political leadership is charged, Smith wrote, with 'promoting the prosperity of the commonwealth, by establishing good discipline, and by discouraging every sort of vice and impropriety'.[2] To neglect this 'exposes the commonwealth to many gross disorders and shocking enormities, and to push it too far is destructive of all liberty, security, and justice'.[3]

Politics is unreceptive to the obvious and simple system of natural liberty. Imagine the politician who stood on the hustings and said, 'Oh, do what you want.'

As for the more successful kind of politicians, Smith addressed their character in a section of *Moral Sentiments* added in 1790:

They have little modesty; are often assuming, arrogant, and presumptuous; great admirers of themselves, and great contemners of other people ... Their excessive presumption, founded upon their own excessive self-admiration, dazzles the multitude ... The frequent, and often wonderful, success of the most ignorant quacks and imposters ... sufficiently demonstrate how easily the multitude are imposed upon by the most extravagant and groundless pretensions.[4]

But – and in politics there is always a but ...

... when those pretensions are supported by a very high
degree of real and solid merit, when they are displayed
with all the splendour which ostentation can bestow upon
them, when they are supported by high rank and great
power ... even the man of sober judgment often abandons
himself to the general admiration.[5]

What may have been most defeating to Smith about politics
was the conundrum of justice and injustice in even the most justifiable political systems. In *The Wealth of Nations*, Smith stated the
requirements for a political order that promotes well-being:

Commerce and manufactures can seldom flourish long in
any state which does not enjoy a regular administration of
justice, in which the people do not feel themselves secure
in the possession of their property, in which the faith of
contracts is not supported by law, and in which the authority of the state is not supposed to be regularly employed in
enforcing the payment of debts.[6]

Justice is necessary for protecting property. But property is
necessarily unjust – 'Wherever there is great property, there
is great inequality.'[7] Smith wrote that we can dispense with
law. 'Where there is no property, ... civil government is not
so necessary.'[8] But then we will get the opposite of law (and
property) in the lawless proprietorship of feudalism or Mao. So
political systems must be established to preserve the injustice
of property by administering justice.

Adam Smith was not an absurdist. Political critiques are better left to a Jonathan Swift or a Bernard Mandeville. In the early 1700s, Mandeville wrote *The Fable of the Bees*, a poem and commentary in which, Mandeville stated, 'I flatter my self to have demonstrated that … what we call Evil in the World, Moral as well as Natural, is the grand Principle that makes us sociable Creatures.'[9]

> *The worst of all the Multitude*
> *Did something for the Common Good.*
>
> …
>
> *… whilst Luxury*
> *Employ'd a Million of the Poor,*
> *And odious Pride a Million more:*
> *Envy it self, and Vanity,*
> *Were Ministers of Industry;*
> *Their darling Folly, Fickleness,*
> *In Diet, Furniture and Dress,*
> *That strange ridic'lous Vice, was made*
> *The very Wheel that turn'd the Trade.*
>
> …
>
> *Thus Vice nurs'd Ingenuity,*
> *Which join'd with Time and Industry,*
> *Had carry'd Life's Conveniences,*
> *It's real Pleasures, Comforts, Ease,*
> *To such Height, the very Poor*
> *Liv'd better than the Rich before,*
> *And nothing could be added more.*[10]

One of Mandeville's other works was *A Modest Defence of Public Stews; or, An Essay upon Whoring*. He was even more poker-faced than Swift in his efforts *pour épater les bourgeois*. This caused Smith to have a sense of humor failure in *Moral Sentiments:* 'There is, however, another system which seems to take away altogether the distinction between vice and virtue, and of which the tendency is, upon that account, wholly pernicious: I mean the system of Dr. Mandeville.'[11]

A 'system which seems to take away altogether the distinction between vice and virtue' – what is that but Poli Sci in thirteen words?

One answer to the political quandary is a populist extension of Smith's obvious and simple liberties. Modern political cynics can at least cite Winston Churchill's dictum from his speech to the House of Commons in November 1947: 'Democracy is the worst form of government, except for all those other forms that have been tried.' But in Smith's time democracy hadn't been tried. Adam Smith had no such touching faith to fall back upon.

There is nothing theoretically wonderful about rule of the people, by the people. For example, in one of Smith's lectures on moral philosophy, he theorized that slavery could never be abolished in a republic because, 'The persons who make all the laws in that country are persons who have slaves themselves.'[12]

Most of the eighteenth century's information about democracy was more than two thousand years old. Like any educated man, Smith knew the history of the Peloponnesian Wars. It's a long story that can be briefly told. Democratic Athens screwed up. Smith didn't consider the more recent experiments in democracy to be encouraging. He looked at Calvinist Protestants in Switzerland and concluded that their 'right of electing their own pastor ... seems to have been productive of nothing but disorder and confusion, and to have tended equally to corrupt the morals both of the clergy and of the people'.[13] (John Calvin had the anti-Trinitarian Michael Servetus burned at the stake in 1553.) Nor was Smith impressed by what he'd seen so far of democracy in the American colonies. He noted the 'rancorous and virulent factions which are inseparable from small democracies',[14] and predicted that if the Americans won their independence, 'those factions would be ten times more virulent than ever.'[15] He thought America's internal disputes 'would probably soon break out into open violence and bloodshed'.[16] Smith was wrong – about 'soon'. It would be eighty-five years before the bombardment of Fort Sumter.

However, if one can't place one's faith in a majority of people, then one has to place one's faith in a minority of them. And Smith did: 'Upon the power which the greater part of the leading men, the natural aristocracy of every country, have of preserving or defending their respective importance, depends the stability and duration of every system of free government.'[17] This trust in a 'natural aristocracy' led Smith into a dangerous, even Latin American, line of reasoning:

Where the military force is placed under the command of those who have the greatest interest in the support of the civil authority, because they have themselves the greatest share of that authority, a standing army can never be dangerous to liberty ... The security which it gives to the sovereign renders unnecessary that troublesome jealousy, which, in some modern republics, seems to watch over the minutest actions, and to be at all times ready to disturb the peace of every citizen.[18]

It's impossible to imagine Adam Smith writing such nonsense about morality or economics. He's got the invisible hand carrying a swagger stick. He's put the Impartial Spectator in a stately home on broad acres. Smith understood how natural liberty works in our ethics and our wallets, but he didn't have a clue how it could operate in the voting booth. When he concocted a recipe for politics he replaced organic natural liberty with processed and genetically modified 'natural aristocracy'.

It's no use criticizing Smith. After 230-odd years of experience we still don't know much about democracy. We have discovered that it works. If you compare the countries that have the greatest degree of democracy with the countries that have the greatest degree of other things we prize, they are the same countries. But an examination of any democratically elected government leads to deep puzzlement about *why* democracy works. And every democratic election produces a dismal display of *how* democracy works. Maybe we the people, with all our idiocies, cancel each other out. Maybe politically empowered people are different from other pests and predators – the only thing worse than a lot of them is a few.

Small doses of politics can make life better, in the way that taking small doses of poison every day was said to make King Mithridates of Pontus immune to poisoning. But politics, as an enterprise, does not lend itself to being part of a project for the betterment of human life. Politics is a different project altogether. Smith knew this. He argued for the distinction between morality and politics in *The Theory of Moral Sentiments:*

> What institution of government could tend so much to
> promote the happiness of mankind as the general prevalence
> of wisdom and virtue? All government is but an imperfect
> remedy for the deficiency of these.[19]

He argued for the distinction between – and the disentanglement of – economics and politics in *The Wealth of Nations:*

> The mean rapacity, the monopolizing spirit of merchants and
> manufacturers, who neither are, nor ought to be, the rulers of
> mankind, though it cannot perhaps be corrected, may very
> easily be prevented from disturbing the tranquillity of any
> body but themselves.[20]

And of politics itself, he declared:

The violence and injustice of the rulers of mankind is an ancient evil, for which, I am afraid, the nature of human affairs can scarce admit of a remedy.[21]

CHAPTER 13

An Inquiry into Adam Smith

Adam Smith did admit of one remedy to the violence and injustice of the rulers of mankind – for mankind to rule itself. He didn't propose democratically selecting our own leaders. They turn out to be violent and unjust anyway. And foolish. They have a dilly of an ego. They have a dally with their staff. They dillydally on issues of national urgency. They listen to their harebrained spouses, obey their raving political advisors, and they get their pictures taken with Gerry Adams and Jack Abramoff. What Smith wanted us to do was use our mental and physical capabilities to render the rulers of mankind as unnecessary and as inconsequential as possible, to leave them in their drafty castles throwing chicken bones on the floor.

In this and other ways Smith's philosophy was solidly based upon and securely fastened to reality. His thoughts could be used. *The Theory of Moral Sentiments* and *The Wealth of Nations* leave the reader with workable rather than ontological (whatever that may mean) ideas. It is as if my Introduction to Philosophy class had dropped Kant's *Critique of Pure Reason* and taken up a critique of my little sister's attachment to that long-haired creep with a motorcycle.

But Smith was a philosopher. *Moral Sentiments* and *Wealth* may offer a program for practical thinking, but they do not offer a practical program. They certainly do not offer a practical political program, as Smith's advice on politics showed.

Philosophy is, I crib from *Webster's Third New International*, definition 4a, 'the sum of an individual's ideas and convictions'. (And, incidentally, you have to read down to 4a before you arrive at a useful definition of philosophy.) There is no need for us to examine the sum of the ideas and convictions of the man who repairs our car, unless he's been convicted of grand theft auto or has an idea that molasses should go in the carburetor. The mechanic's – or even the president's – private life shouldn't much concern us. But a philosopher is different. We have a legitimate interest in knowing what sort of existence the sum of Adam Smith's ideas and convictions resulted in. A man's life doesn't confirm the truth of his thoughts. Men's thoughts about Charlize Theron demonstrate that. But a life is an exhibit of evidence – Exhibit 4a, if you will – in the trial of those thoughts.

This evidence is of special importance in the case of a philosopher who espouses freedom and has the freedom to exercise his own espousal. For example, Jean-Jacques Rousseau, so admired by eight or nine generations now of romantics and radicals, should be indicted. The author of *The Social Contract* kept an illiterate laundress as his mistress and treated her like hell for thirty-three years. Their five children were put in orphanages at birth. Rousseau didn't bother to name them. Smith himself once admired Rousseau, telling a visitor that 'Rousseau conducts the reader to reason and truth by the attractions of sentiment and the force of conviction.'[1] But Smith also wrote a letter from Paris to David Hume about 'this hypocritical Pedant', telling Hume, 'I am thoroughly convinced that Rousseau is as great a Rascal ... as every man here believes him to be.'[2] It is doubtful that Smith allowed himself to be conducted by Rousseau to reason or to truth or to anywhere else without keeping a close eye on the path down which he was being led. It was Rousseau, and definitely not Smith, who wrote, 'Everything is at root dependent on politics.'[3]

Who Adam Smith Really Was, and to What Extent It's None of Our Business

We have good reason to learn about the life of Adam Smith, but there are two problems. The first problem is Smith. He didn't keep a diary. He was a fitful correspondent without much interest in collecting the letters he received. He burned his scholarly notes. He had no toady to write down his every aperçu. He didn't blog.

The second problem is us and what we're used to learning about great men and women or the people who pass for them. What we're used to learning is everything. There is an ongoing biography of Lyndon Johnson, the writing of which is taking a span of time equal to that of LBJ's active political career. And it will take me more than that long to read it. A man's soul is understandable only to God, so the best that mortals can get out of such a purgatorial enterprise is an understanding of the Great Biography Subject's personality.

'Personality' hadn't been invented in the eighteenth century. The Copernican view of the cosmos was accepted. The earth was no longer considered the center of the universe. But Romanticism's neo-Ptolemaic view of the cosmos hadn't come into fashion: the self had not yet taken the earth's place. The bundle of tics and traits and squirrelly notions that make one person different from another was not considered supremely important. Personality, in the 1700s, meant the fact of being a person rather than a thing. The solipsistic motormouth Ralph Waldo Emerson seems to have initiated the use of the word the way we use it.

What an eighteenth-century man had was character. If he possessed any distinctive personal qualities at all, character was the one worth mentioning. As with much that's best in life, character is dull. 'Vice is always capricious: virtue only is regular and orderly,' Smith wrote in *Moral Sentiments*.[4] In Smith's opinion, the 'difference between a man of principle and honour and a worthless fellow' is that 'the one adheres, on all occasions, steadily and resolutely to his maxims, and preserves through the whole of his life one even tenour of conduct. The other, acts variously and accidentally, as humour, inclination, or interest chance to be uppermost.'[5]

Every modern person is a worthless fellow. It's no wonder that many of the most admirable – and unmodern – people of the eighteenth century do not 'come alive on the page' for us moderns. Meanwhile some of the less admirable, like Rousseau, come alive so well that they still need killing off today. Richard Brookhiser coped with this problem of good character in his biography of George Washington, *Founding Father*:

> We worry about our authenticity – about whether our presentation reflects who we 'really' are. Eighteenth-century Americans attended more to the outside story and were less avid to drive putty knives between the outer and inner man. 'Character' ... was a role one played until one became it; 'character' also meant how one's role was judged by others. It was both the performance and the reviews. Every man had a character to maintain; every man was a character actor.[6]

Adam Smith's role as the Fred Mertz in *I Love Political Economy* was as regular and orderly and dull as any proponent of his ideas and defender of his character could hope. Smith lived most of his adult life with his widowed mother, Margaret Douglas Smith, and his spinster cousin, Janet Douglas. They doted on him and he on them. 'And nothing could be added more.'

Smith's comments on his mother, in a letter telling his friend and publisher William Strahan about her death at ninety, are not the stuff of twenty-first-century memoirs: 'a person who certainly loved me more than any other person ever did or ever will love me; and whom I certainly loved and respected more than I ever shall either love or respect any other person'.[7]

Only one domestic anecdote comes down to us, circa 1788, from Sir Walter Scott, who was then an Edinburgh University student. At tea time, said Scott, Smith gave Janet Douglas 'sore confusion, by neglecting utterly her invitation to be seated, and walked round and round ... stopping ever and anon to steal a lump from the sugar basin, which the venerable spinster was at length constrained to place on her own knee, as the only method of securing it from his most uneconomical depredations'.[8] But Sir Walter Scott could make a story out of anything, and often did.

David Douglas, the nine-year-old son of another Smith cousin, was taken into this household when Smith was a bachelor of fifty-five. Skateboards, television, and Xboxes not having been invented, Smith enjoyed this and spent his leisure giving David his lessons. (One hopes 'Variations in the Value of Silver during the Course of the Four last Centuries' was lightly taught.) David Douglas became Smith's heir. Contrary to the heirs-of-the-prominent story line with which we are familiar (what's Scots dialect for *rehab*?), Douglas would ascend to the Scottish bench as Lord Reston.

There is no record of an accusation against Adam Smith for prevarication, deceit, shifty dealing, or even for having a little too much of that good head for business that his esteemed middle class invented. Smith resigned his professorship at Glasgow to tutor the young Duke of Buccleuch. Because Smith left at midterm he tried to return his students' fees. The students liked him so well that none would accept the refund. Smith declared, 'You must not refuse me this satisfaction; nay, by heavens, gentlemen, you shall not.' Then he seized the nearest young man by his coat and stuck the refund in his pocket.[9]

Smith received a life pension for having tutored the Duke of Buccleuch, who called him 'a friend whom I loved and respected, not only for his great talents, but for every private virtue'.[10] Years later the duke helped get a political appointment for Smith, and Smith responded by offering to give up his pension. The only way the duke could talk Smith out of this point of honor was by invoking a more personal point of same. As Smith explained in a letter to a friend, 'His Grace sent me word ... that though I had considered what was fit for my own honour, I had not consider'd what was fit for his; and that he never would suffer it to be suspected that he had procured an office for his friend, in order to relieve himself from the burden of such an annuity.'[11]

Adam Smith made a good living as a member of what he described as 'that unprosperous race of men commonly called men of letters'.[12] And he gave most of it away. One instance came to light in a business letter of Smith's sold at an auction in 1963.[13] Smith explained that two hundred pounds (nine months' worth of his pension) needed to be sent to a 'Welch Nephew' so that the young man wouldn't have to sell his commission in the army. Smith didn't keep a carriage or spend extravagantly on his house or clothes. He entertained with potluck suppers on Sundays. 'The state of his funds at the time of his death, compared with his very moderate establishment, confirmed, beyond a doubt,' wrote an intimate acquaintance, 'what his intimate acquaintances had often suspected, that a large proportion of his annual savings was allotted to offices of secret charity.'[14]

Adam Smith was a big person, with big hands, big teeth, and the big nose everyone in the eighteenth century seems to have had. In his portraits he looks a bit like that other fellow intent upon staying in character, George Washington, but plumper and less denture and democracy afflicted. 'His countenance was manly and agreeable,' said one friend,[15] with, said another, 'a smile of inexpressible benignity'.[16]

There is a disturbing aspect, to a modern reader, about romantic scandals involving Adam Smith: there weren't any. And we have very little information of that type that's unscandalous either. The only biographer of Smith who knew him was Dugald Stewart, occupant of Smith's old chair of moral philosophy at Glasgow University and the son of a Glasgow schoolmate of Smith's. Stewart may be suspected of reticence. He did tell one story:

In the early part of Mr. Smith's life, it is well known to his friends that he was for several years attached to a young lady of great beauty and accomplishment ... What the circumstances were which prevented their union, I have not been able to learn; but I believe it is pretty certain that, after this disappointment, he laid aside all thoughts of marriage. The lady to whom I allude died also unmarried ... I had the pleasure of seeing her when she was turned of eighty, and when she still retained evident traces of her former beauty.[17]

Stewart may also be suspected of sitting up late and reading love poetry.

The author of a more recent (1995) and more thorough-going biography of Smith, Ian Simpson Ross, wrote, 'It is to be feared that the biographer can do little more with the topic of Smith's sex life than contribute a footnote to the history of sublimation.'[18]

But I wouldn't be a truly modern reader if I didn't try. Smith left a couple of hints that he was a man like other men. *The Theory of Moral Sentiments* contains an offhand comment of the kind that men who are like other men always make when fashion's dictates are thwarting nature's inclinations: 'ladies … endeavouring, for near a century past, to squeeze the beautiful roundness of their natural shape into a square form'.[19] And there is that mention in *The Wealth of Nations* of the potato-fed 'unfortunate women who live by prostitu-tion' whom Smith called 'the most beautiful women perhaps in the British dominions'.[20] Let modern readers supply a 'hmmm'.

While with the Duke of Buccleuch on grand tour in France, Smith was set upon by a French marquise, said by Smith's nineteenth-century biographer, John Rae, to be 'bent upon mak-ing so famous a conquest'.[21] It was all Smith could do to fend her off, which embarrassed Smith and amused the members of his traveling party. But this may not have been a matter of chastity alone. A friend told a friend that the real reason Smith fought shy of the marquise was his love for an English lady staying in the same town. This seems to have resulted in a disappointment additional to the one described by Dugald Stewart. Perhaps Smith renounced marriage forever more than once. Men have been known to.

Anyway Smith did make a conquest, of the heart if not the rest of Mme Riccoboni in Paris. She was a famous actress who quit the stage to become a more famous author of romantic novels. She wrote a letter to her friend the playwright and actor David Garrick, a letter which John Rae and other Smith biographers as late as the 1960s discreetly left in French:

> Oh these Scotts! These Scottish dogs! They come to please me and afflict me! I am like those silly young girls who listen to a lover without thinking of regret, always the neighbor of pleasure. Scold me, beat me, kill me! But I love Mr. Smith, I love him very much. I would like the devil to carry away all our literary minds, our philosophers, and bring back Mr. Smith.[22]

Not to be outdone in effusiveness (though an effusiveness of a very Scots kind) Smith included Mme Riccoboni in his revision of *The Theory of Moral Sentiments:*

> The poets and romance writers, who best paint the refinements and delicacies of love and friendship, and of all other private and domestic affections, Racine and Voltaire; Richardson, Maurivaux, and Riccoboni; are, in such cases, much better instructors than Zeno, Chrysippus, or Epictetus.[23]

An update of Smith's list being something like 'Stoppard, Pinter, Updike, Bellow, and Danielle Steele'.

However it was that, in the Enlightenment, character out-weighed personality, Smith had plenty of the latter. We'd be inclined to set aside his character and just call him one. He talked to himself. His head swayed continually from side to side. When he walked he looked as though he was headed off in all directions. He told friends that once, as he passed along the High Street in Edinburgh, he heard a market woman tsk-tsk about an obviously prosperous lunatic being allowed to wander alone.

Smith was splendidly absentminded. While he was working on *The Wealth of Nations* at his mother's house in Kirkcaldy, he is supposed to have gone out into the garden in his dressing gown and, lost in thought, wandered into the road. He walked to Dumferline, fifteen miles away, before steeple bells broke his reverie and he realized he was wearing his robe and slippers in the midst of a crowd going to church.

Someone who breakfasted with Smith in London said that Smith, deeply involved in a conversation, put bread and butter and boiling water into a teapot, served himself, and pronounced it the worst cup of tea he'd ever had. Smith was avoided as a whist partner by his fellow professors at Glasgow University because if he got an idea during a game he would claim he had no more cards in the suit being played. Dining at Dalkeith House, the country seat of the Duke of Buccleuch, Smith be-gan a scathing commentary on some important politician with the politician's closest relative sitting across the table. Smith stopped when he realized this. But then he began talking to himself, saying that the devil may care but it was all true.

Most of these anecdotes fall into the journalist's category of 'too good to check'. But there is evidence of their general truth in the student notes taken during Smith's Glasgow lectures on rhetoric. Smith mentioned an absentminded character in a French play, and scribbled into the notebook margin is a Latin tag to the effect of 'Look who's talking.'

When Smith was a government official in Edinburgh he had a ceremonial guard consisting of a porter dressed in an elaborate military-style tunic and wielding a seven-foot staff. Each day when Smith arrived the porter would perform a sort of drill team exercise. One day Smith became fascinated by this and, using his bamboo cane in place of the staff, matched the porter's every motion, present arms for present arms, about face for about face, parade rest for parade rest. Afterward no one could convince Smith that he'd done anything odd. Dugald Stewart says Smith had an aesthetic theory that much of the pleasure we get from the imitative arts has to do with the dif-ficulty of the imitation. Maybe that's what Smith was thinking about. Or maybe he was just having a goof.

As absent as Smith's mind was, he was present. He thought highly enough of sociability that he included it in his section on propriety in *Moral Sentiments:* 'Society and conversation ... are the most powerful remedies for restoring the mind to its tranquillity.'[24] He belonged to a profusion of clubs, from the Royal Society of London to something called the Select Society of Edinburgh, which debated things such as the ideal size of farms in Scotland and offered a prize to anyone who could 'cure the greatest number of smokey chimneys'. He was even made an honorary captain of the Edinburgh city guard, though whether before or after his performance with the porter I don't know.

Smith must have been a likable man. John Rae tells a story of a French professor of geology being subjected by Smith to an evening of bagpipe music. It was, in the words of the geology professor, 'a most hideous noise'. But afterward the same Frenchman reported that 'there was nobody in Edinburgh he visited more frequently than Smith.'[25]

Smith knew David Hume, Edward Gibbon, Pitt the Younger, Sir Walter Scott, Voltaire, Rousseau, Edmund Burke, James Watt, Benjamin Franklin, and le Duc de La Rochefoucauld. It's impossible today to imagine knowing a range of such people. There are no such people.

Smith's closest friendship was with David Hume, whom he met in Edinburgh in about 1750. They were a sort of high-minded, very intellectual Laurel and Hardy without the tantrums or pie throwing, or a Hardy and Hardy since neither was skinny or laconic. A passage in *Moral Sentiments* seems to be the straight man's version of the relationship:

> But of all the attachments to an individual, that which is founded altogether upon the esteem and approbation of his good conduct and behaviour, confirmed by much experience and long acquaintance, is, by far, the most respectable …
> The attachment which is founded upon the love of virtue,

as it is certainly, of all attachments, the most virtuous; so it is likewise the happiest, as well as the most permanent and secure.[26]

For the Hume version, there is an elaborate set piece, a twelve-hundred-word comic routine in a letter, written from London, to Smith who was in Glasgow awaiting news of how the publication of *The Theory of Moral Sentiments* had been received. Hume lists every important person to whom he's given a copy and provides biographical details of them before saying,

> I have delayd writing to you till I cou'd tell you something of the Success of the Book, and coud prognosticate with some Probability whether it shoud be finally damnd to Oblivion, or shoud be registerd in the Temple of Immortality. Tho' it has been publishd only a few Weeks, I think there appear already such strong Symptoms, that I can almost venture to fortell its Fate. It is in short this – But I have been interrupted in my Letter by a foolish impertinent Visit of one who has lately come from Scotland. He tells me, that the University of Glasgow intend to declare Rouets Office Vacant ... ,

Hume then expends a long paragraph on gossip about who might get this post, leading to gossip about mutual acquaintances and a digression on their friend Lord Kames and his book *Historical Law-Tracts*, of which Hume says,

A man might as well think of making a fine Sauce by a Mixture of Wormwood and Aloes as an agreeable Composition by
joining Metaphysics and Scotch Law ... But to return to your
Book, and its Success in this Town, I must tell you – A Plague
of Interruptions! I orderd myself to be deny'd; and yet here
is one that has broke in upon me again. He is a man of Letters, and we have had a good deal of literary Conversation.
You told me, that you was curious of literary Anecdotes, and
therefore I shall inform you of a few ...

Which Hume does.

But what is all this to my Book? say you. – My Dear
Mr. Smith, have Patience: Compose yourself to Tranquillity:
Show yourself a Philosopher in Practice as well as Profession:
Think on the Emptiness, and Rashness, and Futility of the
common Judgements of Men: How little they are regulatd by
Reason in any Subject, much more in philosophical Subjects,
which so far exceed the Comprehension of the Vulgar.

An apposite Latin quotation is inserted followed by a string
of further admonishments to equanimity and a story about
how the Athenian politician Phocion always suspected
that he'd made a mistake when he was applauded by the populace. 'Supposing, therefore,' wrote Hume, 'that you have duely
prepard yourself for the worst by all these Reflections; I proceed
to tell you the melancholy News, that your Book has been
very unfortunate; For the Public seem disposd to applaud it

extremely. It was lookd for by the foolish People with some Impatience; and the Mob of Literati are beginning already to be very loud in its Praises.'[27]

In this book, which the mob of literati were loudly praising, Adam Smith wrote that he believed 'the chief part of human happiness arises from the consciousness of being beloved.'[28] Smith was not, however, one of those dreadful individuals of whom it is said, 'He was beloved by all.' Dr Johnson didn't like him. Supposedly they had their first encounter at a party in London, and later that evening Smith turned up at another party saying of Johnson, 'He's a brute; he's a brute.' Johnson had attacked Smith for defending Hume's character despite Hume's atheistic views, and Smith had persisted in championing Hume.

'What did Johnson say?' Smith was asked.

'He said, "You lie."'

'What did you say?'

'I said, "You are a son of a bitch."'[29]

This story seems to be not quite true. But let it stand for what transpires from the meeting of the greatest minds of an age.

Apparently Smith and Johnson did have some sort of unpleasant exchange. When Boswell informed Johnson that Smith detested blank verse, Johnson said, 'Sir, I was once in company with Smith, and we did not take to each other, but had I known that he loved rhyme as much as you tell me he does, I should have hugged him.'*[30]

---

*Boswell had been a fawning student of Smith's at Glasgow but later turned cheeky. After David Hume's death Smith wrote a eulogy saying, 'I

But they must have made it up because Smith became a member of the Literary Club where Dr Johnson was the cynosure. And Johnson defended *The Wealth of Nations,* saying, 'A man who has never been engaged in trade himself may undoubtedly write well upon trade, and there is nothing that requires more to be illustrated by philosophy than does trade.'[31]

Adam Smith's Life – A Very Economical Sketch

Adam Smith was born sometime early in 1723, the posthumous son of another Adam Smith who had been judge advocate for Scotland and the comptroller of customs in the Kirkcaldy district. A libertarian Freudian, if there is such, could make something of Smith Junior's psychological attitude toward free trade.

His family was reasonably prosperous and reasonably well connected. He spent his childhood in Kirkcaldy, across the Firth of Forth from Edinburgh. His one great adventure happened when he was four. He was stolen by gypsies, though rather anticlimactically found a couple of hours later. Smith biographer John Rae wrote, 'He would have made, I fear, a

have always considered him … as approaching as nearly to the idea of a perfectly wise and virtuous man, as perhaps the nature of human frailty will permit' (CAS 221). Boswell took Christian umbrage at this, called it 'daring effrontery', and bragged, 'Surely, now have I more understanding than my teachers' (Rae 312).

Sadly, Smith may have been partly to blame for the Boswells of this world and their never-ending tell-alls. Boswell claimed that Smith, in his rhetoric lectures, said that there was nothing too frivolous to be learned about a great man, that Smith said he was glad to know that Milton wore latchets on his shoes and not buckles. (Rae 371) poor gipsy.'[32] I'm not so sure. Instead of telling fortunes and hatching confidence schemes, today's gypsies might be running Citicorp.

Smith attended a little village school in Kirkcaldy that seems to have been somewhat different than the little village school my children attend. Smith began studying Latin at ten. But I doubt he knew how to play 'Kumbayah' on the recorder or to scold his mother for not recycling. At fourteen he was sent to study at Glasgow University, college freshmen being that age in those days. This gave them some excuse for acting like college freshmen, though we have no evidence that Smith did.

Smith's favorite subject was mathematics, which either makes sense or it doesn't, depending on how you think the math works out in a free market economy. Smith's favorite teacher, however, was Francis Hutcheson, philosopher, ethicist, and one of those luminaries of the Scottish Enlightenment whose light is nowadays under the bushel of intellectual history. Hutcheson was the first professor at Glasgow to lecture in English instead of Latin. He was a strong advocate of personal liberty and of the economic part of that liberty, which we take so personally. It was Hutcheson, not Jeremy Bentham, who first declared that the determining factor in morality was 'the greatest happiness of the greatest number'.* [33]

Smith was partly indebted to Hutcheson for the thesis that the right to property is based on labor. (John Locke had made

---

*Leaving aside Plato, *The Republic*, book 4: 'our aim in founding the State was not the disproportionate happiness of any one class, but the greatest happiness of the whole.'

a similar argument.) Hutcheson believed man had a right to property because he had a right to benefit from the labor used on that property. And Hutcheson indirectly gave Smith the idea for the Impartial Spectator. Hutcheson concluded that sympathy couldn't be the basis of morality because we often approve of actions taken by people with whom we don't sympathize. Smith saw a way around that argument.

During Smith's first year at the university, Glasgow's Presbyterian clergy tried to excommunicate Hutcheson. He was considered too religiously optimistic, teaching that God gave us ways to know good from evil even if we weren't religious. The fray was survived by Hutcheson, but seems to have impressed Smith. In his works Smith was always averse to religious controversy and, indeed, to religion, but at the same time he managed to be, in his own way, always religiously optimistic.

Smith received a Snell Exhibition, a sort of Rhodes Scholarship of its day, allowing him to attend Oxford University. Smith had been a frail child, and his health was never very good, but he wasn't a wimp. He rode a horse 350 aching miles from Glasgow to Oxford.

He hated the place. 'In the university of Oxford,' he wrote in *The Wealth of Nations*, 'the greater part of the public professors have, for these many years, given up altogether even the pretence of teaching.'[34] Smith spent his time in reading that was extensive even by Smithian standards. He read works in Latin, Greek, French, Italian, and English. Smith, who'd been in correspondence with David Hume – although they'd yet to meet – was caught reading Hume's *A Treatise of Human Nature*.

This was confiscated by the Tory dons. His stay in Oxford from age seventeen to twenty-three was the only time in Smith's life when he seems to have made no friends.

In 1746 he gave up his Snell Exhibition and went home to live with his mother. He earned his keep giving paid lectures on English literature. Smith liked Pope and Gray and didn't like Milton's shorter, more readable poems. He believed Dryden was a better poet than Shakespeare and agreed with Voltaire that Shakespeare had written good scenes but not a good play. In the preface to *Lyrical Ballads*, Wordsworth would call Smith 'the worst critic, David Hume excepted, that Scotland, a soil to which this sort of weed seems natural, has produced'.[35]

Smith himself may not have thought too highly of the lectures. There's a comment in *The Theory of Moral Sentiments* about certain things being 'merely a matter of taste' and having 'all the feebleness and delicacy of that species of perceptions'.[36] Among the self-betterers of Edinburgh, part of the attraction of the lectures was the English rather than the literature. Smith was listened to as someone who had fashionably lost his Scots accent. It is a good thing for us that he did, or reading *The Wealth of Nations* would be like attending the worst kind of Robert Burns recital.

In 1751, when he was twenty-eight, Smith was appointed professor of logic at Glasgow University. He was soon promoted to the more prestigious chair of moral philosophy. Smith was a popular professor. Dr Tronchin, Voltaire's physician, sent his son to study under Smith, and the future prime minister, Lord Shelburne, sent his younger brother. Besides the likes of James

Boswell, Smith attracted students from as far as Russia. Semyon Efimovich Desnitsky and Ivan Andreyevich Tret'yakov would become professors at the University of Moscow, where they preached the ideas of Adam Smith. These did not catch on.

At Glasgow, Smith also served as quaestor, curator of the college chambers, vice rector, praeses of the university meetings, and in other funnily named administrative posts. By all accounts he was trusted and effective. There's an important difference between absentminded and scatterbrained – the difference, for example, between the foreign policies of Britain and France.

Smith called his tenure at Glasgow University 'the period of 13 years which … I remember as by far the most useful and therefore as by far the happiest and most honourable period of my life'.[37] Although Smith wrote that in a letter thanking the university for electing him rector in 1787, and what else would he say? Also, there's the 'therefore' to be considered.

In 1763, Smith was offered a position as tutor, to accompany the seventeen-year-old Duke of Buccleuch to France. And he accepted readily enough.

Smith's opinion of such continental tours was recorded in *The Wealth of Nations:*

> In England, it becomes every day more and more the custom to send young people to travel in foreign countries immediately upon their leaving school … Our young people, it is said, generally return home much improved by their travels. A young man who goes abroad at seventeen

or eighteen, and returns home at one and twenty, returns
three or four years older ... At that age it is very difficult
not to improve a good deal in three or four years ... In other
respects, he commonly returns home more conceited, more
unprincipled, more dissipated, and more incapable of any
serious application either to study or to business, than he
could well have become in so short a time, had he lived at
home.[38]

The Duke of Buccleuch seems to have been a nice young
man. He grew up to be, according to the eleventh edition of
The Encyclopaedia Britannica, 'famous for his generosity and
benefactions', not the least of which were to Adam Smith. It is
to be hoped that Smith was generalizing and/or trusted that
the duke would never read *Wealth*.

Smith's job opportunity came from the duke's stepfather,
Charles Townshend, the future chancellor of the exchequer,
who would kick off the American Revolution with his Tea Duties. But *The Wealth of Nations* hadn't been written. Townshend
was impressed with Smith's first book.

Moral Sentiments also impressed the French. Smith was received in all the most intellectual of salons, although his ability
to speak the language was wretched. Perhaps there was a lot
of note passing to Quesnay, Turgot, Helvétius, Diderot, and,
of course, Mme Riccoboni. If her letter to Garrick is anything
to go by, we can imagine the kind of notes she passed back.

On a trip to Geneva, Smith met with Voltaire five or six times.
Apparently Voltaire told Smith a story about how their mutual

friend, the old reprobate Duc de Richelieu, had borrowed the embassy plate at Vienna and never returned it. And Voltaire remarked to Smith, as he remarked to others, that 'the English have only one sauce, melted butter.' Meeting of Great Minds, Part II. The French professor who endured the bagpipe music said Smith revered the memory of Voltaire.

At the end of 1766, Smith returned home and went to work in earnest on *The Wealth of Nations*. The book had had its beginnings in a fit of boredom in Toulouse – a better response to the tedium of that city than setting fire to cars in its suburbs. Smith wrote and rewrote for the next ten years.

The publication of *Wealth* had immediate effects, not necessarily good ones. Book 5 was what the men of influence seized upon. Any advice given to government, no matter how reasonable, intelligent, or well principled, has only one result – more government. In 1777 and 1778 the prime minister, Lord North, introduced four new taxes, all suggested, probably inadvertently, by Smith.

There was a tax on menservants, who were engaged in what Smith had categorized as 'unproductive labour', and a tax on inhabited houses because Smith had said, 'The rent of houses is paid for the use of an unproductive subject.'[39] There was a tax on property sold at auction. Smith had unfortunately mentioned that certain property transfers are 'either public and notorious, or ... cannot be long concealed' and that 'such transactions, therefore, may be taxed directly.'[40] And there was a tax on malt, which meant a tax on beer, that luxurious expense of the inferior ranks of people. Smith's intentions had been good. He'd merely pointed out, in his consideration of 'Taxes upon consumable Commodities', that 'a greater revenue than what is at present drawn from all the heavy taxes upon malt, beer, and ale, might be raised … by a much lighter tax upon malt.'[41] But we know what road it is that good intentions pave, and it's not the road to cheap beer.

The Wealth of Nations had some good effects as well, such as the entire modern free world. Smith's arguments helped shape the Treaty of Paris, ending the Revolutionary War. The Earl of Shelburne, whose younger brother had boarded at Smith's house at Glasgow University, was an early adapter. He claimed to have been converted to Smith's ideas during a trip the two took from Glasgow to London in 1761. Shelburne became prime minister in 1782. The next year he signed the peace with the United States. Shelburne claimed that the Treaty of Paris was inspired by 'the great principle of free trade' and that 'a peace was good in the exact proportion that it recognized that principle.'[42]

Four years later Pitt the Younger would evoke the same Smithian principle in his Consolidation Bill reforming Britain's customs and excise laws. Centuries of mercantilist expedients and government grasps at revenue had caused these regulations to grow to the point that 2,537 individual resolutions were required to present the provisions of the Consolidation Bill to Parliament. Pitt also tried to effect Smith's idea of constitutional union with Ireland. The quarrel resulting from that is still going on.

There is a story that a few years before Smith died he went to a house in London where a distinguished company was gathered, including the Lord Advocate Henry Dundas, Privy Councillor William Grenville, Bishop William Wilberforce, Pitt, and Henry Addington who would follow Pitt as prime minister. They all rose when Smith entered the room.

'Be seated, gentlemen,' said Smith.

'No,' replied Pitt, 'we will stand till you are first seated, for we are all your scholars.'[43]

It may have happened. But how the politicians of the world really viewed Adam Smith was probably better expressed by the Tory Pitt's longtime political rival Charles James Fox. It was Fox, not Pitt, who supposedly shared Smith's Whig convictions – political liberalization, social tolerance, support of parliamentary authority over royal prerogative. Fox was one of those *bien-pensant* progressives with messy personal lives, the Ted Kennedy type, who was very in favor of the French Revolution and very opposed to British intervention in the French revolutionary wars and so on. Fox told the author and memoirist Charles Butler that he had never read *The Wealth of Nations* and explained, 'There is something in all these subjects which passes my comprehension; something so wide that I could never embrace them myself nor find any one who did.'[44]

Therefore, naturally, as any student of politics could predict, it was Fox who first cited *The Wealth of Nations* in Parliament. And his citation indicates the perfect truth of what Fox told Butler:

There was a maxim laid down in an excellent book upon the Wealth of Nations ... which was indisputable as to its truth.

In that book it was stated that the only way to become rich
was to manage matters so as to make one's income exceed
one's expenses. This maxim applied equally to an individual
and to a nation.[45]

The political system gave Adam Smith an appropriate com-
pensation, the way the political systems so often reward us for
our sins. In 1778, Smith was made a commissioner of customs
for Scotland, with a large salary and various prerequisites such
as that marching porter at the Customs House door.

Between book sales and the commissionership, Smith was
making money with efforts to eliminate customs duties and with
efforts to collect them. He wouldn't have thought it was as funny
as we do. It was the family business. Not only had Smith's father
been comptroller of customs in Kirkcaldy, but so had a cousin,
a third Adam Smith, who went on to hold the customs office
of Inspector General of the Outports. Also, there was a history
of incompetence and peculation in the British customs service.
Setting a fox to watch the geese – if it was a very theoretical,
honest, and disinterested (and not Charles Fox) fox – was better
than the usual practice of setting a goose to watch them.

After seven years as a commissioner, Smith wrote to William
Eden, secretary of the Board of Trade, that 'the net revenue
arising from the Customs of Scotland is at least four times
greater than it was seven or eight years ago ... I flatter myself
it is likely to increase still further.'[46]

At the same time it's unlikely that Smith was a ferocious
presence on the customs bench. He thought of excessive

import duties as a sort of entrapment and wrote in *The Wealth of Nations*, 'The law, contrary to all the ordinary principles of justice, first creates the temptation, and then punishes those who yield to it.'[47] Smith expressed concern that smuggling, rather than ruining the economy, would 'ruin the smuggler; a person who, though no doubt highly blameable for violating the laws of his country, is frequently incapable of violating those of natural justice, and would have been, in every respect, an excellent citizen, had not the laws of his country made that a crime which nature never meant to be so'.[48] Smith even went so far as declaring that, 'to pretend to have any scruple about buying smuggled goods, ... [was] one of those pedantic pieces of hypocrisy which, instead of gaining credit with any body, serve only to expose the person who affects to practise them, to the suspicion of being a greater knave than most of his neighbours.'[49] The old ladies in the charter bus at the Niagara Falls border crossing, with their purses full of Canadian prescription drugs, would be treated kindly by Adam Smith.

As were his mother and spinster cousin whom he moved into an attractive house in Edinburgh. There he lived the last twelve years of his life, busily and sociably, according to the program he recommended to the working men of England and Scotland in book 1 of *Wealth*:

> Great labour, either of mind or body, continued for several days together, is in most men naturally followed by a great desire of relaxation ... It is the call of nature, which

requires to be relieved by some indulgence, sometimes of ease only, but sometimes too of dissipation and diversion.[50]

Nature made its last call on July 17, 1790. Smith's health had worsened. In his last revisions to *Moral Sentiments* he added two dozen paragraphs, mostly approving, on the Stoic attitude toward death: 'Walk forth without repining; without murmuring or complaining. Walk forth calm, contented, rejoicing, returning thanks to the Gods, who, from their infinite bounty, have opened the safe and quiet harbour of death, at all times ready to receive us from the stormy ocean of human life.'[51] Smith had grown thin and weak, but on the Sunday before he died he hosted the customary weekly supper for his friends. His last recorded words were, 'I believe we must adjourn this meeting to some other place.'[52]

CHAPTER 14

Adam Smith in Heaven

To what sort of place was Adam Smith proposing to adjourn? That is, what was this 'pure and rational religion, free from every mixture of absurdity, imposture, or fanaticism', which he and the rest of the wise men wished to see established? Wouldn't its funerals be dull without absurdity? And what kind of wedding ceremony lacks imposture? We know – sometimes in excruciating detail – what Adam Smith thought. What Adam Smith believed is harder to determine.

Smith is generally lumped in with much of the Enlightenment intelligentsia and called a Deist – someone who thought all God did was wind the universe's clock. Hit the snooze button, please. John Rae called Smith, more precisely, a Theist. The difference being that Theism emphasizes belief in God while Deism emphasizes disbelief in the supernatural aspects of religion, which, broadly considered, are all the aspects religion has. Smith believed in a more actively involved God: 'the very suspicion of a fatherless world, must be the most melancholy of all reflections.'[1] Although we all know how actively involved fathers often are in child care.

Smith frequently depersonalized God by using the word *nature*. Frequently, but not always. In *The Theory of Moral Sentiments*, Smith, having written that 'the works of nature ... seem all intended to promote happiness, and to guard against misery',[2] went on to state that when we impede those works of nature, we 'declare ourselves, if I may say so, in some measure the enemies of God'.[3]

To what extent Adam Smith was a proper Christian is even harder to determine. And, after all, it's a Christian article of faith that nobody is one. A gossipy contemporary of Smith's, John Ramsay of Ochtertyre, called Smith 'ominously reticent' on religious subjects and said he was seen openly smiling during divine service. (Aren't we supposed to?) I can find only one direct mention of Jesus Christ in the works Smith published, and that in passing, '... our Saviour's precept ...'[4] But it's respectful, and it's capitalized. One-third of the Holy Trinity went unexamined by Adam Smith. (Between nature and the Impartial Spectator, he paid plenty of attention to the other two-thirds.) Yet our Savior also went unattacked. It's possible that Smith thought the importance of Christianity went without saying.

If so, this wasn't enough for fervent Christians. In the final edition of *Moral Sentiments*, Smith deleted a long theological paragraph full of Christian justification for divine retribution. This editing, combined with Smith's praise of Hume, caused muscular Christians of the nineteenth century metaphorical steroid rage. Reportedly Smith said the passage that offended by omission was cut because it was 'unnecessary and misplaced'.[5] It was. Smith's topic was our personal desire for retribution, a subject that's anything but divine. If Adam Smith were alive he'd still be offending. For example, Smith would almost certainly point out that evolution *is* intelligent design.

Smith repeatedly stated his uninterest in metaphysics. But when Smith became a professor at Glasgow University he signed the Westminster Confession of Faith, affirming the creed of the Presbyterian Church. Presumably the signature was still valid when he accepted the title of rector thirty-six years later. Adam Smith wouldn't have been the first person to hold secretly conventional religious opinions – or to have found them boring to think about. 'Nature,' he wrote, 'has not prescribed to us this sublime contemplation as the great business and occupation of our lives.'[6]

All that is not to say Smith wasn't a religious skeptic, only that he was so skeptical that it's entirely possible he was skeptical of skepticism, too.

Smith was possessed of a deeply unconvinced logic. 'Convicted but not convinced' was a phrase he was heard to mutter to himself after losing a debate at one of his clubs in Glasgow.[7] If he did not reject religion, he rejected religiosity and protested as foolish that 'the public and private worship of the Deity, have been represented, even by men of virtue and abilities, as the sole virtues which can either entitle to reward or exempt from punishment in the life to come.'[8]

Smith did not believe in asceticism and 'those whining and melancholy moralists, who are perpetually reproaching us with our happiness'.[9] He had his doubts about stoicism and 'the perfect apathy which it prescribes to us, by endeavouring, not merely to moderate, but to eradicate all our private, partial, and selfish affections'.[10] He called this 'a stupid insensibility to the events of human life'.[11]

Smith respected Hume but wondered about the utilitarian ideas that Hume held. Smith wrote that if we embraced utilitarianism 'we should have no other reason for praising a man than that for which we commend a chest of drawers.'[12]

And Smith particularly distrusted every form of casuistry and the sly and ugly reasoning it uses to get virtue into the Procrustes' bed of self-justification. Smith wrote that the man who needs to consult the casuists – or as we call them, the lawyers, public relations experts, lobbyists, and campaign spin doctors – 'was the man of equivocation and mental reservation, the man who seriously and deliberately meant to deceive, but who, at the same time, wished to flatter himself that he had really told the truth'.[13]

Smith was not very impressed with most philosophers. And he was very unimpressed with some, paraphrasing Cicero in his comment, 'There is nothing so absurd … which has not sometimes been asserted by some philosophers.'[14]

'Philosophers,' Smith wrote, 'are apt to cultivate with a peculiar fondness, as the great means of displaying their ingenuity, the propensity to account for all appearances from as few principles as possible.'[15] He used Epicurus as his example, but he hardly could have helped thinking about himself. In Smith's opinion there was something conceited about philosophy: 'Men are fond of paradoxes, and of appearing to understand what surpasses the comprehension of ordinary people.'[16] And there was something ultimately beside the point about philosophy: 'The reasonings of philosophy ... though they may confound and perplex the understanding, can never break down the necessary connection which Nature has established between causes and their effects.'[17] Smith considered even reason itself to have a dubious side: 'It is altogether absurd and unintelligible to suppose that the first perceptions of right and wrong can be derived from reason.'[18]

Adam Smith set out to do a monumental piece of work, to construct something that would help improve every aspect of existence. Skepticism isn't usually considered to be a kit of building tools. Socrates may have been the only other philosopher who attempted to craft a good thing with skepticism, if you consider Plato a good thing. Adam Smith, in fact, did: 'The humane Plato ... with all that love of mankind which seems to animate all his writings'.[19] But there's nothing in *The Wealth of Nations* like the Oceana and Utopia absurdities in *The Republic*, with its 'hymns to the gods and praises of famous men are the only poetry which ought to be admitted into our State' (book 10). And although Adam Smith was a skeptic, *The Wealth of Nations* and *The Theory of Moral Sentiments* do not contain any of the gross pessimism that marked such ancient skeptics as Pyrrho of Elis, Arcesilaus, and Aenesidemus (who may have been pessimistic because they rightly supposed nobody would bother to preserve their works or remember their names).

Skepticism was just Adam Smith's way of not bothering to look at things that can't be seen. He could see that mankind had sympathy, imagination, and a desire to get on in the world. And he could see that all sorts of what he called 'speculative systems' stood in mankind's way. It was on these speculative systems that Smith labored with his tools of skepticism, grinding eyeglass prescriptions for excessively farsighted visionary schemes, erasing too-precise dimensions in blueprints for society, and letting the air out of philosophy with a single well-chosen synonym for metaphysics, 'Pneumatics'.[20] Smith wrote:

> Speculative systems have in all ages of the world been adopted for reasons too frivolous to have determined the judgment of any man of common sense, in a matter of the smallest pecuniary interest. Gross sophistry has scarce ever had any influence upon the opinions of mankind, except in matters of philosophy and speculation; and in these it has frequently had the greatest.[21]

Take care of the pennies, and the speculative philosophers, the utopians, the politicians, the economists, and God will take care of themselves.

An Adam Smith Philosophical Dictionary

Any consideration of the works of Adam Smith leaves a lot that remains to be considered. There is no room in this small book about Smith's great book for all, or even many, of Smith's adages, aphorisms, epigrams, insights, observations, maxims, axioms, judicious perceptions, and prejudiced opinions.* Voltaire, who in some ways inspired Adam Smith, gathered his brief hortatory writings into something he called the *Dictionnaire Philosophique*. When Voltaire's literary executors were compiling a complete edition of his works they found themselves confronted with all sorts of literary odds and ends – pamphlets, screeds, short essays, manuscript notes, and so forth. They purloined Voltaire's title and packed these items into the *Dictionnaire*, creating a hodgepodge that was hardly a dictionary and was philosophical only in the broadest sense. A further crib of the Voltaire notion seems a reasonable (and easy) method for organizing the intellectual leftovers from an attempt to make a meal of Adam Smith's thought.

*In the following entries a few liberties have been taken with Smith's texts. Independent clauses sometimes have been turned into complete sentences. A number of 'buts' and 'howevers' that refer to preceding material have been removed along with a few other extraneous words. Ellipses have been inserted only where substantive omissions have been made.

Banking, Islamic
When the law prohibits interest altogether, it does not prevent it.

– *Wealth*, book 1[1]

Business and Government, the Visionary Link between Them
Avarice and injustice are always shortsighted.

– *Wealth*, book 3[2]

Business, Government Regulation of
To be merely useless is perhaps the highest eulogy which can ever justly be bestowed upon a regulated company.

– *Wealth*, book 5[3]

Career Counseling, Futility of
The over-weening conceit which the greater part of men have of their own abilities, is an ancient evil remarked by the philosophers and moralists of all ages. Their absurd presumption in their own good fortune, has been less taken notice of ... The contempt of risk and the presumptuous hope of success, are in no period of life more active than at the age at which young people chuse their professions.

– *Wealth*, book 1[4]

'Caring'
Let us suppose that the great empire of China, with all its myriads of inhabitants was suddenly swallowed up by an

earthquake, and let us consider how a man of humanity in Europe ... would be affected upon receiving intelligence of this dreadful calamity. He would, I imagine, first of all, express very strongly his sorrow for the misfortune of that unhappy people, he would make many melancholy reflections upon the precariousness of human life ... And when all this fine philosophy was over, when all these humane sentiments had been once fairly expressed, he would pursue his business or his pleasure, take his repose or his diversion, with the same ease and tranquillity, as if no such accident had happened ... If he was to lose his little finger to-morrow, he would not sleep to-night; but ... he will snore with the most profound security over the ruin of a hundred millions of his brethren.

– *Moral Sentiments*, part 3[5]

Celebrity, Allure of Being a

The man of rank and distinction is observed by all the world. Every body is eager to look at him, and to conceive, at least by sympathy, that joy and exultation with which his circumstances naturally inspire him ... Scarce a word, scarce a gesture, can fall from him that is altogether neglected ... He has, every moment, an opportunity of interesting mankind, and of rendering himself the object of the observation and fellow-feeling of every body about him. It is this, which ... notwithstanding the loss of liberty with which it is attended, renders greatness the object of envy.

– *Moral Sentiments*, part 1[6]

Celebrity, How a Fading One Is Compelled to Act Up
For though to be overlooked, and to be disapproved of, are things entirely different, yet as obscurity covers us from the daylight of honour and approbation, to feel that we are taken no notice of, necessarily … disappoints the most ardent desire, of human nature.

– Moral Sentiments, part 1[7]

Celebrity, Last Word upon
This disposition to admire, and almost to worship, the rich and the powerful, and to despise, or, at least, to neglect persons of poor and mean condition … is the great and most universal cause of the corruption of our moral sentiments.

– Moral Sentiments, part 1[8]

Clothes, Advice to Work-Shy Young Layabouts Wearing Silly
As it is ridiculous not to dress, so is it not to be employed, like other people.

– Wealth, book 1[9]

Colbert, Jean-Baptiste, Louis XIV's Finance Minister,
His Misapprehension about the Similarity of Business
to Government, Which Was Opposite to – Yet Identical
with – Donald Rumsfeld's
The industry and commerce of a great country he endeavoured to regulate upon the same model as the departments of a public office.

– Wealth, book 4[10]

Confession
No man applies to his confessor for absolution, because he did not perform the most generous, the most friendly, or the most magnanimous action which, in his circumstances, it was possible to perform.

– Moral Sentiments, part 7[11]

Consumer Rights, First Known Statement of
The interest of the producer ought to be attended to, only so far as it may be necessary for promoting that of the consumer.

– Wealth, book 4[12]

Corporations, Governance of
The trade of a joint stock company is always managed by a court of directors ... subject, in many respects, to the control of a general court of proprietors. But the greater part of these proprietors seldom pretend to understand any thing of the business of the company; and ... give themselves no trouble about it, but receive contentedly such half yearly or yearly dividend, as the directors think proper to make to them ... The directors of such companies, however, being the managers rather of other people's money than of their own, it cannot well be expected, that they should watch over it with the same anxious vigilance with which the partners in a private co-partnery frequently watch over their own. Like the stewards of a rich man, they are apt to consider attention to small matters as not for their master's honour, and very easily

give themselves a dispensation from having it. Negligence and profusion, therefore, must always prevail, more or less.

– Wealth, book 5[13]

Credit Cards, Complaints about Interest Payments on
As something can every-where be made by the use of money, something ought every-where to be paid for the use of it.

– Wealth, book 2[14]

Culture, Popular
Music and dancing are the great amusements of almost all barbarous nations.

– Wealth, book 5[15]

Culture, Popular, Continued
All savages are too much occupied with their own wants and necessities, to give much attention to those of another person.

– Moral Sentiments, part 5[16]

Culture, Popular, Further Thoughts upon
Drowsy stupidity, in a civilized society, seems to benumb the understanding of almost all the inferior ranks of people.

– Wealth, book 5[17]

Drugs, Why Laws Against Them Don't Work
(and Why I'm So Late Getting Home)
It is not the multitude of ale-houses ... that occasions a general disposition to drunkenness among the common people; but

that disposition arising from other causes necessarily gives employment to a multitude of ale-houses.

– Wealth, book 2[18]

EU

The policy of Europe, no-where leaves things at perfect liberty.

– Wealth, book 1[19]

Economics, the Two Reasons for Its Existence, Italics Added
Political œconomy, considered as a branch of the science of a statesman or legislator, proposes two distinct objects: first, to provide a plentiful revenue or subsistence for the people, *or more properly to enable them to provide such a revenue or subsistence for themselves;* and secondly, to supply the state or commonwealth with a revenue *sufficient* for the public services.

– Wealth, book 4[20]

Economics, the Other Two Reasons for Its Existence,
Italics Unnecessary
The cheapness of consumption and the encouragement given to production, precisely the two effects which it is the great business of political œconomy to promote.

– Wealth, book 5[21]

Effectual Demand
A very poor man may be said in some sense to have a demand for a coach and six; ... but his demand is not an effectual demand.

– Wealth, book 1[22]

Enemies, Primitive Indigenous, Plus ça Change …
Nothing can be more contemptible than an Indian war in North America.

– *Wealth*, book 5[23]

Famine
Whoever examines, with attention, the history of the dearths and famines which have afflicted any part of Europe, during either the course of the present or that of the two preceding centuries … will find … that a famine has never arisen from any other cause but the violence of government attempting, by improper means, to remedy the inconveniencies of a dearth.

– *Wealth*, book 4[24]

Famine, Avoidance of
After the trade of the farmer, no trade contribut[es] so much to the growing of corn as that of the corn merchant.

– *Wealth*, book 4[25]

Fart Jokes
It is often more mortifying to appear in public under small disasters, than under great misfortunes.

– *Moral Sentiments*, part 1[26]

Fashion Victims
In every civilized society … there have been always two different schemes or systems of morality current at the same time; of which the one may be called the strict or austere; the other

the liberal, or, if you will, the loose system. The former is generally admired and revered by the common people: the latter is commonly more esteemed and adopted by what are called people of fashion.

– Wealth, book 5[27]

Free Enterprise, the Unpolitical Power of
Though the profusion of government must, undoubtedly, have retarded the natural progress of England towards wealth and improvement, it has not been able to stop it.

– Wealth, book 2[28]

Good Cheer, Its Relationship to the National
Current Account Deficit
To attempt to increase the wealth of any country, either by introducing or by detaining in it an unnecessary quantity of gold and silver, is as absurd as it would be to attempt to increase the good cheer of private families, by obliging them to keep an unnecessary number of kitchen utensils.

– Wealth, book 4[29]

Greed, Why It Really Is Good and How a Greedy Mind
Destroys Monopolistic Combinations among Merchants
and Manufacturers
In a free trade an effectual combination cannot be established but by the unanimous consent of every single trader, and it cannot last longer than every single trader continues of the same mind.

– Wealth, book 1[30]

Hate Crimes, Prosecution for
Sentiments, thoughts, intentions, would become the objects of punishment ... Every court of judicature would become a real inquisition. There would be no safety for the most innocent and circumspect conduct. Bad wishes, bad views, bad designs, might still be suspected.

– *Moral Sentiments*, part 2 [31]

Hilton, Paris, the Numerous Feuds of, Explained
Rivalship and emulation render excellency, even in mean professions, an object of ambition, and frequently occasion the very greatest exertions.

– *Wealth*, book 5 [32]

Homeless, an Alternative View on the
The beggar, who suns himself by the side of the highway, possesses that security which kings are fighting for.

– *Moral Sentiments*, part 4 [33]

Husbands
It is the interest of every man to live as much at his ease as he can; and if his emoluments are to be precisely the same, whether he does, or does not perform some very laborious duty, it is certainly his interest ... either to neglect it altogether, or, if he is subject to some authority which will not suffer him to do this, to perform it in as careless and slovenly a manner as that authority will permit.

– *Wealth*, book 5 [34]

Husbands, Continued

To seem not to be affected with the joy of our companions is but want of politeness; but not to wear a serious countenance when they tell us their afflictions, is a real and gross inhumanity.

– *Moral Sentiments*, part 1[35]

Immigration, Excessive Worries about

A man is of all sorts of luggage the most difficult to be transported.

– *Wealth*, book 1[36]

Interior Decoration, Novel Suggestion for

Trophies of the instruments of music or of agriculture, imitated in painting or in stucco, make a common and an agreeable ornament of our halls and dining-rooms. A trophy of the same kind, composed of the instruments of surgery, of dissecting and amputation-knives, of saws for cutting bones, ... etc. would be absurd and shocking.

– *Moral Sentiments*, part 1[37]

Italy

Italy still continues to command some sort of veneration by the number of monuments which it possesses, though the wealth which produced them has decayed, and though the genius which planned them seems to be extinguished.

– *Wealth*, book 2[38]

Limousine Liberals, Explanation for

The owners of great capitals ... have generally either some direct share, or some indirect influence, in the administration of government. For the sake of the respect and authority which they derive from this situation, they are willing to live in a country where their capital ... will bring them less profit.

– *Wealth*, book 5[39]

Limousine Liberals, Real Explanation for

In public, as well as in private expences, great wealth may, perhaps, frequently be admitted as an apology for great folly.

– *Wealth*, book 4[40]

Living Standards, Modern

The accommodation of a European prince does not always so much exceed that of an industrious and frugal peasant, as the accommodation of the latter exceeds that of many an African king, the absolute master of the lives and liberties of ten thousand naked savages.

– *Wealth*, book 1[41]

Malthus, Thomas, Refuted

The most decisive mark of the prosperity of any country is the increase of the number of its inhabitants.

– *Wealth*, book 1[42]

Malthus, Thomas, Refuted Again

The demand for men, like that for any other commodity, necessarily regulates the production of men.

– *Wealth*, book 1[43]

Monarchy or Democracy, Which Is Worse?

England … in time of peace, has generally conducted itself with
the slothful and negligent profusion that is perhaps natural to
monarchies; and in time of war has constantly acted with all
the thoughtless extravagance that democracies are apt to fall
into.

– *Wealth*, book 5[44]

Money

Money … is a steady friend.

– *Wealth*, book 4[45]

Money, a Steady Friend When We Can Find Him

When we have money we can more readily obtain whatever
else we have occasion for, than by means of any other commodity. The great affair, we always find, is to get money.

– *Wealth*, book 4[46]

Nuclear Proliferation, Bright Side of

Hereafter … the inhabitants of all the different quarters of the
world may arrive at that equality of courage and force which,
by inspiring mutual fear, can alone overawe the injustice of

independent nations into some sort of respect for the rights of one another.

– *Wealth*, book 4[47]

Off-Broadway Play, Idea for
The loss of a leg may generally be regarded as a more real calamity than the loss of a mistress. It would be a ridiculous tragedy, however, of which the catastrophe was to turn upon a loss of that kind.

– *Moral Sentiments*, part 1[48]

Planning, Central, Nature of in USSR Foreseen
The fear of punishment can never be a motive of sufficient weight to force a continual and careful attention to a business.

– *Wealth*, book 5[49]

Politics, Inherent Evil of Explained
It is unjust that the whole society should contribute towards an expence of which the benefit is confined to a part of the society.

– *Wealth*, book 5[50]

Poor, but Happy
The vices of levity are always ruinous to the common people.

– *Wealth*, book 5[51]

Presidents, Ex-
Of all the discarded statesmen who for their own ease have studied to get the better of ambition, and to dispise those

honours which they could no longer arrive at, how few have been able to succeed?

– Moral Sentiments, part 1[52]

Presidents, Ex-, Continued

With what impatience does the man of spirit and ambition, who is depressed by his situation, look round for some great opportunity to distinguish himself? ... He even looks forward with satisfaction to the prospect of foreign war, or civil dissension.

– Moral Sentiments, part 1[53]

Pride and Vanity, in Defense of

Pride is frequently attended with many respectable virtues ... Vanity, with many amiable ones.

– Moral Sentiments, part 6[54]

Quality, Guarantees of

Quality is so very disputable a matter, that I look upon all information of this kind as somewhat uncertain.

– Wealth, book 1[55]

Reagan, Ronald, Original Source of a Phrase Popularly Attributed to

[Re: the East India Company] ... waste which the fraud and abuse, inseparable from the management of the affairs of so great a company, must necessarily have occasioned.

– Wealth, book 4[56]

Rich, the

With the greater part of rich people, the chief enjoyment of riches consists in the parade of riches, which in their eye is never so complete as when they appear to possess those decisive marks of opulence which nobody can possess but themselves.

– *Wealth*, book 1[57]

Riche, the Nouveau

Their wealth would alone excite the public indignation, and the vanity which almost always accompanies such upstart fortunes, the foolish ostentation with which they commonly display that wealth, excites that indignation still more.

– *Wealth*, book 5[58]

Ruin, National

Be assured, there is a great deal of ruin in a nation.

– Smith, to a young man who'd brought him the news of the British defeat at Saratoga, saying the nation must be ruined[59]

Santa Claus, Why We Tell Children There Is a

There seems to be in young children an instinctive disposition to believe whatever they are told. Nature seems to have judged it necessary for their preservation that they should ... put implicit confidence in those to whom the care of their childhood ... is entrusted. Their credulity, accordingly, is excessive, and it requires long and much experience of the falsehood of mankind to reduce them to a reasonable degree of diffidence and distrust.

– *Moral Sentiments*, part 7[60]

Scholars

Before the invention of the art of printing, a scholar and a beggar seem to have been terms very nearly synonymous.

– *Wealth*, book 1[61]

Shopping

What is over and above satisfying the limited desire, is given for the amusement of those desires which cannot be satisfied, but seem to be altogether endless.

– *Wealth*, book 1[62]

Social Security Explained

[In ancient Athens] children were acquitted from maintaining those parents in their old age, who had neglected to instruct them in some profitable trade or business.

– *Wealth*, book 5[63]

Statistics, Everything You Need to Know
about the Government's

I have no great faith in political arithmetic.

– *Wealth*, book 4[64]

Success, Pro and Con

Power and riches ... are enormous and operose machines ... consisting of springs the most nice and delicate, which must be kept in order with the most anxious attention, and which in spite of all our care are ready every moment to burst into pieces, and to crush in their ruins their unfortunate possessor ...

The pleasures of wealth and greatness ... strike the imagination as something grand and beautiful and noble, of which the attainment is well worth all the toil and anxiety which we are so apt to bestow upon it. And it is well that nature imposes upon us in this manner. It is this deception which rouses and keeps in continual motion the industry of mankind.

– *Moral Sentiments*, part 4[65]

Televangelists

Mendicant friars, whose beggary being not only licensed, but consecrated by religion, [are] a most grievous tax upon the poor people.

– *Wealth*, book 4[66]

Televangelists, Success vs. Mainstream Protestant Clergy

Such a clergy, when attacked by a set of popular and bold, though perhaps stupid and ignorant enthusiasts, feel themselves as perfectly defenceless as the indolent, effeminate, and full-fed nations of the southern parts of Asia, when they were invaded by the active, hardy, and hungry Tartars of the North.

– *Wealth*, book 5[67]

Tourists, the Kind Who Come Home Raving about the
Excellence of Mass Transportation in Other Countries
In China, ... the high roads, and still more the navigable canals,
it is pretended, exceed very much every thing of the same kind
which is known in Europe. The accounts of those works, however, which have been transmitted to Europe, have generally
been drawn up by weak and wondering travellers; frequently
by stupid and lying missionaries.

– *Wealth*, book 5[68]

UN
The regard for the laws of nations, or for those rules which independent states profess or pretend to think themselves bound
to observe in their dealings with one another, is often very little
more than mere pretence and profession.

– *Moral Sentiments*, part 6[69]

Veracity, Legislative
The printed debates of the House of Commons [are] not always
the most authentic records of truth.

– *Wealth*, book 5[70]

Verse, Blank
They do well to call it blank, for blank it is. I myself even, who
never could find a single rhyme in my life, could make blank
verse as fast as I could speak.

– Smith, to an anonymous
newspaper interviewer[71]

Virtue, Economic Analysis of
The late resolution of the Quakers in Pennsylvania to set at liberty all their negro slaves, may satisfy us that their number cannot be very great.

– *Wealth*, book 3[72]

Wages, Too Low Compared to Profits
The demand for those who live by wages … naturally increases with the increase of national wealth, and cannot possibly increase without it.

– *Wealth*, book 1[73]

Wages, Too High Compared to Profits
The liberal reward of labour … to complain of it, is to lament over the necessary effect and cause of the greatest public prosperity.

– *Wealth*, book 1[74]

War, as an Economic Stimulus without Which We
Would Be Better Off
In the midst of the most destructive foreign war, … the greater part of manufactures may frequently flourish greatly; and, on the contrary, they may decline on the return of the peace. They may flourish amidst the ruin of their country, and begin to decay upon the return of its prosperity.

– *Wealth*, book 4[75]

War, Public Fondness for

In great empires the people who live in the capital, and in the provinces remote from the scene of action, feel, many of them, scarce any inconveniency from the war; but enjoy, at their ease, the amusement of reading in the newspapers the exploits of their own fleets and armies. To them this amusement compensates the small difference between the taxes which they pay on account of the war, and those which they had been accustomed to pay in time of peace. They are commonly dissatisfied with the return of peace, which puts an end to their amusement.

– *Wealth*, book 5[76]

War, Smith's Plan for Curtailment of

Were the expence of war to be defrayed always by a revenue raised within the year, … wars would in general be more speedily concluded, and less wantonly undertaken.

– *Wealth*, book 5[77]

Wives

The fair-sex, who have commonly much more tenderness than ours, have seldom so much generosity.

– *Moral Sentiments*, part 4[78]

CAS   *Correspondence of Adam Smith*. Edited by E. C. Mossner and I. S. Ross. Oxford, 1977. Liberty Fund, 1987.

DS   Stewart, Dugald. *Collected Works*. Vol. 10, *Biographical Memoirs of Adam Smith, William Robertson, Thomas Reid*. Edinburgh: T. Constable, 1858.

EPS   *Essays on Philosophical Subjects*. Edited by W. P. D. Wightman and J. C. Bryce. Oxford, 1980. Liberty Fund, 1982.

ISR   Ross, Ian Simpson. The Life of Adam Smith. Oxford: Oxford University Press, 1995.

LJ   *Lectures on Jurisprudence*. Edited by R. L. Meek, D. D. Raphael, and P. G. Stein. Oxford, 1978. Liberty Fund, 1982.

Rae   Rae, John. *Life of Adam Smith*. London: Macmillan, 1895.

TMS   *The Theory of Moral Sentiments*. Edited by D. D. Raphael and A. L. Macfie. Oxford: Oxford University Press, 1976. Reprint, Indianapolis: Liberty Fund, 1982.

TRTS   Hayek, Friedrich A. von. *The Road to Serfdom*. Chicago: University of Chicago Press, 1944.

West   West, E. G. *Adam Smith*. New Rochelle, N.Y.: Arlington House, 1969.

W/L   *An Inquiry into the Nature and Causes of the Wealth of Nations* (2 vols.), edited by R. H. Campbell and A. S. Skinner, Oxford, 1976; Liberty Fund, 1981.

W/ML   *An Inquiry into the Nature and Causes of the Wealth of Nations.* Edited by Edwin Cannan. New York: Modern Library, 1937.

Chapter 1

   1. W/ML 715
   2. W/ML 90
   3. DS 52
   4. TMS 226
   5. W/L 782
   6. W/ML lix

Chapter 2

   1. W/ML 932
   2. W/L 124
   3. TMS 28
   4. West 111
   5. Rae 269
   6. W/ML 214
   7. W/ML 552
   8. W/ML 467
   9. CAS 387
   10. W/ML 148
   11. W/L 388
   12. W/ML xliii

Chapter 3

   1. W/L 471
   2. W/ML 584
   3. EPS 105
   4. Ibid.
   5. TMS 82
   6. TMS 9
   7. TMS 16
   8. TMS 9
   9. TMS 106
   10. TMS 304

11. TMS 137
12. Ibid.
13. TMS 247
14. TMS 86
15. Ibid.
16. TMS 142
17. TMS 241
18. TMS 25
19. TMS 184
20. TMS 118
21. TMS 25
22. TMS 219
23. TMS 272
24. W/ML 14
25. TMS 77
26. TMS 292

Chapter 4

1. W/ML 15
2. Ibid.
3. W/ML 140
4. Ibid.
5. Ibid.
6. W/ML 99
7. W/L 14
8. Rae 286
9. W/ML 28
10. W/ML 47
11. W/ML 36–7
12. W/ML 39
13. W/ML 47
14. W/ML 95
15. W/ML 250
16. W/ML 61
17. Ibid.
18. W/ML 56
19. W/ML 76
20. W/ML 113
21. W/ML 287
22. W/ML 288
23. W/L 570

24. W/ML 87
25. W/ML 274
26. W/ML 63
27. Ibid.
28. W/ML 95
29. W/ML 89
30. W/ML 279
31. W/ML 287
32. W/ML 42
33. W/ML 188
34. TMS 184–5
35. TMS 57
36. TMS 234
37. W/L 48
38. W/ML 162

Chapter 5

1. W/ML 304–5
2. W/ML 321
3. LJ/352
4. W/ML 314
5. W/ML 32
6. W/ML 349
7. W/ML 335–6
8. W/ML 110
9. W/ML 359
10. W/ML 353
11. Ibid.
12. W/ML 348
13. W/ML 314
14. Ibid.
15. W/ML 349
16. Ibid.
17. W/ML 350
18. W/ML 345
19. LJ 518
20. W/ML 355–6
21. W/ML 353
22. W/ML 552
23. W/ML 423
24. W/ML 341

25. W/ML 343
26. Ibid.
27. W/ML 345
28. Ibid.

Chapter 6

1. W/ML 372
2. W/ML 376
3. W/ML 376–7
4. W/ML 360
5. W/ML 361
6. Ibid.
7. Ibid.
8. W/ML 372
9. W/ML 381
10. W/ML 319
11. W/ML 19
12. W/ML 320
13. W/ML 306
14. W/ML 843
15. W/ML 838
16. Ibid.
17. W/ML 146
18. W/ML 145
19. W/ML 145–6
20. TRTS 55
21. W/ML 391
22. W/ML 365
23. W/ML 366
24. W/ML 365–6
25. W/ML 309
26. Ibid.
27. Ibid.
28. W/ML 394
29. W/ML 395
30. Ibid
31. Ibid.
32. W/ML 397
33. Ibid.
34. W/ML 399
35. W/ML 406

36. W/ML 374–5
37. W/ML 803–4
38. W/ML 804
39. LJ 570
40. W/ML 373–4
41. W/L 19

Chapter 7

1. W/ML 409
2. TMS 57
3. W/ML 413
4. Ibid.
5. W/ML 440
6. W/ML 414
7. W/ML 443
8. W/ML 31
9. Alexander Carlyle, *Anecdotes and Characters of Our Times*, quoted in Arthur Herman, *How the Scots Invented the Modern World* (New York: Crown, 2001), 122.
10. W/ML 415
11. W/ML 416
12. Ibid.
13. Ibid.
14. W/ML 363
15. Jane Austen, *Pride and Prejudice*, Chapter 13.
16. W/ML 417
17. Ibid.
18. W/ML 417–18
19. W/ML 418
20. W/ML 427
21. Ibid.
22. Ibid.
23. W/ML 428–9
24. W/ML 429
25. W/ML 440
26. W/ML 430
27. Ibid.
28. W/ML 440
29. W/ML 444–5
30. W/ML 446–7
31. W/ML 447

Chapter 8

1. W/ML 552
2. W/ML 456–7
3. W/ML 467
4. W/ML 461
5. W/ML 530
6. W/ML 521
7. W/ML 498
8. W/ML 485
9. W/ML 629
10. W/ML 738
11. W/ML 737
12. W/ML 498
13. W/ML 496
14. W/ML 319
15. W/ML 458
16. W/ML 479
17. W/ML 530
18. W/ML 528
19. W/ML 526
20. W/ML 409
21. W/ML 421
22. W/ML 569
23. W/ML 531–2
24. W/ML 532
25. W/ML 581

Chapter 9

1. W/ML 723
2. W/ML 725
3. W/ML 724
4. W/ML 726
5. W/ML 731
6. W/ML 745
7. W/ML 736
8. TMS 185
9. TMS 232
10. Ibid.
11. Ibid.
12. TMS 233–4

13. TMS 187

14. W/ML 728

15. W/ML 735

16. David Hume to the Abbé André Morellet, London, July 10, 1769, in *The Letters of David Hume*, vol. 2, *1766–1776*, ed. J. Y. T. Greig (Oxford: Oxford University Press, 1932), 205. Morellet was a philosopher and a friend of Voltaire.

Chapter 10

1. V. I. Lenin, 'Imperialism, the Highest Stage of Capitalism,' quoted in Thomas Sowell, *Marxism: Philosophy and Economics* (New York: Morrow, 1985), 213.

2. V. I. Lenin, *Imperialism*, International Publishers, 1939, p. 13, quoted by Thomas Sowell, ibid.

3. David Hume, 'The Sceptic', in *Essays, Moral, Political, and Literary* (Indianapolis: Liberty Classics, 1987), 169.

4. W/ML 1026

5. CAS 383

6. CAS 380–1

7. CAS 384

8. CAS 383

9. W/ML 636

10. W/ML 556

11. W/ML 477

12. W/ML 637

13. W/ML 636

14. W/ML 660

15. W/ML 629

16. Ibid.

17. W/ML 663, 665

18. W/ML 618–19

19. CAS 381

20. W/ML 672

21. W/ML 666

22. Ibid.

23. Ibid.

24. CAS 382

25. W/ML 1013

26. CAS 382

27. Ibid.
28. W/ML 675
29. W/ML 1028
30. Ibid.

Chapter 11

1. TMS 291
2. Ibid.
3. W/ML 633
4. W/ML 858
5. W/ML 774
6. W/ML 771–2
7. W/ML 771
8. W/ML 766
9. Ibid.
10. W/ML 766–7
11. W/ML 767
12. W/ML 768
13. Ibid.
14. W/ML 769
15. W/ML 770
16. W/ML 778
17. W/ML 776
18. W/ML 782
19. W/ML 780
20. W/ML 785–6
21. W/ML 775
22. W/ML 791
23. W/ML 781
24. W/ML 831
25. W/ML 829
26. W/ML 829–30
27. W/ML 827
28. W/ML 830
29. W/ML 821
30. W/ML 822
31. W/ML 839
32. W/ML 824
33. Ibid.

34. W/ML 855
35. W/ML 839
36. W/ML 855
37. W/ML 832
38. W/ML 857
39. W/ML 849
40. W/ML 849–50

41. In this section of *Wealth*, Smith includes a lengthy quotation from David Hume, *The History of England, from the Invasion of Julius Caesar to the Revolution in 1688*, vol. 4 (London: T. Caddell, 1773), 30–31. In his own footnote, Smith says that the 1773 edition 'differs verbally both from earlier and from later editions'.

42. W/ML 850
43. W/ML 867
44. W/ML 852
45. Ibid.
46. Ibid.
47. W/ML 854
48. W/ML 862
49. W/ML 888
50. Ibid.
51. W/ML 889
52. W/ML 970
53. W/ML 929
54. W/ML 914
55. Ibid.
56. W/ML 909
57. W/ML 907
58. W/ML 919
59. W/ML 934
60. Ibid
61. Ibid.
62. W/ML 935
63. W/ML 958
64. W/ML 945
65. W/ML 278
66. W/ML 185
67. W/ML 941
68. W/ML 923
69. W/ML 909
70. W/ML 980

71. W/ML 880
72. W/ML 997
73. W/ML 1008
74. W/ML 1012
75. W/ML 1009
76. W/ML 765
77. W/ML 669
78. W/ML 745
79. Ibid.

Chapter 12

1. TMS 35
2. TMS 81
3. Ibid.
4. TMS 249
5. TMS 249–50
6. W/ML 985
7. W/ML 766
8. W/ML 767
9. Bernard Mandeville, *The Fable of the Bees*, vol. 1, (Oxford: Oxford University Press, 1924), 369.
10. Ibid., 24, 25, 26.
11. TMS 308
12. LJ 181
13. W/ML 868
14. W/ML 1025–6
15. W/ML 1026
16. Ibid.
17. W/ML 671
18. W/ML 763–4
19. TMS 187
20. W/ML 527
21. Ibid.

Chapter 13

1. Rae 372
2. CAS 112–13
3. Quoted in Paul Johnson, *Intellectuals* (London: Weidenfeld & Nicolson, 1988), 26.

4. TMS 225
5. TMS 163
6. Richard Brookhiser, *Founding Father: Rediscovering George Washington* (New York, Free Press, 1996), 131–2.
7. CAS 275
8. ISR 310
9. Rae 170
10. ISR 227
11. CAS 252–3
12. W/ML 152
13. CAS 269
14. DS 72
15. ISR 311
16. ISR 416
17. DS 97
18. ISR 214
19. TMS 199
20. W/ML 185
21. Rae 213
22. Rae 211; ISR 210; West 146
23. TMS 143
24. TMS 23
25. Rae 372, 374
26. TMS 224–5
27. CAS 33–5
28. TMS 41
29. Rae 156
30. Rae 35
31. Rae 288
32. Rae 5
33. Rae 12
34. W/ML 821
35. Rae 34
36. TMS 193
37. West 204
38. W/ML 832
39. W/ML 907
40. W/ML 925
41. W/ML 960
42. Rae 383
43. Rae 405

44. Rae 289
45. Rae 290
46. West 187–8
47. W/ML 889–90
48. W/ML 970
49. Ibid.
50. W/ML 94
51. TMS 280
52. Rae 435

Chapter 14

1. TMS 235
2. TMS 166
3. Ibid.
4. TMS 178
5. TMS 384
6. TMS 292
7. Rae 96
8. TMS 132
9. TMS 139
10. TMS 292
11. TMS 244
12. TMS 188
13. TMS 339
14. W/ML 945
15. TMS 299
16. W/ML 642
17. TMS 293
18. TMS 320
19. TMS 210
20. W/ML 829
21. W/ML 828

Appendix

1. W/ML 110
2. W/ML 422–3
3. W/ML 793
4. W/ML 124, 126
5. TMS 136

6. TMS 51
7. Ibid.
8. TMS 61
9. W/ML 96–7
10. W/ML 719
11. TMS 334
12. W/ML 625
13. W/ML 800
14. W/ML 387
15. W/ML 834
16. TMS 205
17. W/ML 840
18. W/ML 392
19. W/ML 115
20. W/ML 455
21. W/ML 808
22. W/ML 63
23. W/ML 749
24. W/ML 563
25. W/ML 570
26. TMS 60
27. W/ML 746
28. W/ML 376
29. W/ML 468
30. W/ML 148–9
31. TMS 105
32. W/ML 820
33. TMS 185
34. W/ML 821
35. TMS 15
36. W/ML 86
37. TMS 35–6
38. W/ML 379
39. W/ML 980
40. W/ML 559
41. W/ML 13
42. W/ML 80
43. W/ML 92
44. W/ML 880
45. W/ML 457
46. W/ML 456
47. W/ML 676

48. TMS 29
49. W/ML 798
50. W/ML 877
51. W/ML 853
52. TMS 57
53. TMS 55
54. TMS 258
55. W/ML 244
56. W/ML 681–2
57. W/ML 198
58. W/ML 976
59. CAS 262n
60. TMS 335
61. W/ML 152
62. W/ML 188–9
63. W/ML 835
64. W/ML 573
65. TMS 182–3
66. W/ML 620
67. W/ML 847
68. W/ML 688
69. TMS 228
70. W/ML 797
71. Rae 35
72. W/ML 418
73. W/ML 79
74. W/ML 93
75. W/ML 473
76. W/ML 996
77. W/ML 878
78. TMS 190

BIBLIOGRAPHY

The best way to read Adam Smith is in the Glasgow editions, commissioned by the University of Glasgow to celebrate the 1976 bicentennial of the publication of *The Wealth of Nations*. A group of preeminent Smith scholars applied themselves to the complete body of Adam Smith's work, including what was recorded of his lectures, and handsomely introduced and annotated it. A separate index covers the multitude of persons and subjects upon which Adam Smith touched. These eight volumes were issued in hardcover by the Oxford University Press. They are also available in paperback from the Liberty Fund in Indianapolis, Indiana. The Liberty Fund editions are exact photographic reproductions of the Oxford books.

I did not, alas, use the Glasgow edition of *Wealth* for my primary reading. I already had a 1937 Modern Library version that I'd owned for almost forty years and that was dog-eared and underlined (in what - it is to be admitted, few - parts of it I'd read). My Modern Library edition is not without merits. It has a hilarious Marxist introduction by the late wind-bag Max Lerner. More to the point it was edited by Edwin Cannan, and includes his editor's introduction, footnotes, and marginal summaries, all of them excellent. Cannan was perhaps the greatest of all Adam Smith textual authorities - so much so that the text resulting from the very careful editing of the Glasgow edition differs hardly at all from what Cannan produced in 1904.

The Modern Library still has *Wealth* in print, minus the Marxism. My poor old book has been read to pieces. But I've found another copy from 1937, its dust cover still intact. Here I see that this Modern Library Giant, as it was called, was decorated with a charcoal drawing in socialist realist style on a Bolshevist red background showing some workers of the world very pointlessly yanking a rope. It is to be hoped that the reader has not felt similarly employed with what he or she now holds in hand.

Works of Adam Smith

Modern Library Editions

An Inquiry into the Nature and Causes of the Wealth of Nations. Edited by Edwin Cannan. New York: Modern Library, 1937.

The Wealth of Nations. Edited, with an Introduction and Notes by Edwin Cannan. New York: Modern Library, 1994.

The Glasgow Editions

The Theory of Moral Sentiments. Edited by D. D. Raphael and A. L. Macfie. Oxford: Oxford University Press, 1976. Reprint, Indianapolis: Liberty Fund, 1982.

An Inquiry into the Nature and Causes of the Wealth of Nations. Edited by R. H. Campbell and A. S. Skinner. 2 vols. Oxford, 1976. Liberty Fund, 1981.

Essays on Philosophical Subjects. Edited by W. P. D. Wightman and J. C. Bryce. Oxford, 1980. Liberty Fund, 1982.

Lectures on Rhetoric and Belles Lettres. Edited by J. C. Bryce. Oxford, 1983. Liberty Fund, 1985.

Lectures on Jurisprudence. Edited by R. L. Meek, D. D. Raphael, and P. G. Stein. Oxford, 1978. Liberty Fund, 1982.

Correspondence of Adam Smith. Edited by E. C. Mossner and I. S. Ross. Oxford, 1977. Liberty Fund, 1987.

Index to the Works of Adam Smith. Compiled by K. Haakonssen and A. S. Skinner. Oxford, 2001. Liberty Fund, 2001.

Other Books and Articles

Boaz, David, ed. *The Libertarian Reader.* New York: Free Press, 1997.

Buchholz, Todd G. *New Ideas from Dead Economists.* New York: New American Library, 1989.

Campbell, R. H., and A. S. Skinner. *Adam Smith.* New York: St Martin's, 1982.

Friedman, Milton. *Capitalism and Freedom.* Chicago: University of Chicago Press, 1962.

Friedman, Milton, and Rose Friedman. *Free to Choose.* New York: Harcourt Brace Jovanovich, 1980.

Fry, Michael, ed. *Adam Smith's Legacy.* London: Routledge, 1992.

Greenspan, Alan, 'Adam Smith.' Adam Smith Memorial Lecture, Kirkcaldy, Scotland, February 6, 2005. Washington, DC: Federal Reserve Board, 2005. http://www.federalreserve.gov/boarddocs/speeches/2005/20050206/default.htm (accessed August 28, 2006).

Hayek, Friedrich A. von. *The Road to Serfdom.* Chicago: University of Chicago Press, 1944.

Hazlitt, Henry. *Economics in One Lesson.* New York: Harper & Brothers, 1946.

Herman, Arthur. *How the Scots Invented the Modern World.* New York: Crown, 2001.

Johnson, Paul. *Intellectuals.* London: Weidenfeld & Nicolson, 1988.

Mandeville, Bernard. *The Fable of the Bees.* 2 vols. Oxford: Oxford University Press, 1924.

Pipes, Richard. *Property and Freedom.* New York: Knopf, 1999.

Rae, John. *Life of Adam Smith.* London: Macmillan, 1895.

Raphael, D. D. *Adam Smith.* Oxford: Oxford University Press, 1985.

Ross, Ian Simpson. *The Life of Adam Smith.* Oxford: Oxford University Press, 1995.

Ryan, Edward W. *In the Words of Adam Smith.* Sun Lakes, Ariz.: Thomas Horton, 1990.

Salerno, Joseph T. 'Carl Menger: The Founder of the Austrian School.' Auburn, Ala.: Ludwig von Mises Institute, 2005. http://www.mises. org/content/mengerbio.asp (accessed August 28, 2006).

Samuelson, Paul A., and William D. Nordhaus. *Economics.* 15th edn. New York: McGraw-Hill, 1995.

Sowell, Thomas. *Marxism: Philosophy and Economics.* New York: Morrow, 1985.

Stewart, Dugald. *Collected Works.* Vol. 10, *Biographical Memoirs of Adam Smith, William Robertson, Thomas Reid.* Edinburgh: T. Constable, 1858.

Tufte, Edward R. *The Visual Display of Quantitative Information.* 2nd edn. Cheshire, Conn.: Graphics Press, 2001.

Weatherford, Jack. *The History of Money.* New York: Crown, 1997.

West, E. G. *Adam Smith.* New Rochelle, NY: Arlington House, 1969.

White, T. H. *The Age of Scandal.* London: Jonathan Cape, 1950.

Williams, Jonathan, ed. *Money: A History.* London: British Museum Press, 1997.

Yardeni, Edward E., and David A. Moss. 'The Triumph of Adam Smith.' Topical Study 19. New York: Prudential-Bache Securities, 1990. http://www.adamsmith.org/smith/triumph-of-smith.pdf (accessed August 28, 2006).